# The Clever
# COOKBOOK

## Get-Ahead Strategies and Timesaving Tips for Stress-Free Home Cooking

RECIPES AND PHOTOGRAPHY BY

## Emilie Raffa

WWW.THECLEVERCARROT.COM

PAGE STREET
PUBLISHING CO.

PAGE STREET
PUBLISHING CO.

First published in 2016 by

Page Street Publishing Co.

27 Congress Street, Suite 103

Salem, MA  01970

www.pagestreetpublishing.com

Distributed by Macmillan, sales in Canada by The Canadian Manda Group.


19   18   17   16      1   2   3   4   5


ISBN-13: 978-1-62414-216-1

ISBN-10: 1-62414-216-8


Library of Congress Control Number:  2015950623


Cover and book design by Page Street Publishing Co.

Photography by Emilie Raffa


Printed and bound in the United States

Page Street is proud to be a member of 1% for the Planet. Members donate one percent of their sales to one or more of the over 1,500 environmental and sustainability charities across the globe who participate in this program.

This Book Is Dedicated to My Family

# Contents

# INTRODUCTION

Let's face it: The problem with cooking, is *cooking*.

It wasn't until I had kids, and basically no free time, that I realized putting a homemade meal on the table was a constant struggle. There were nights I dined on Rice Krispies and was perfectly okay with that. There are *still* nights I reach for a box of cereal or bottom-feed off my kids' leftover PB&Js. But at some point, my habits had to stop. Not only was it detrimental to myself, it wasn't a good example to set for my family. And the irony of it all? I went to culinary school.

But change for the better wasn't always easy.

My youngest was born with colic and screamed and cried for six weeks straight. There was no putting him down, no showering, none of that stuff. I thought about food to keep me sane. As a distraction, I learned how to bake sourdough, studied photography and scribbled down recipes on junk mail. This noisy time in my life turned out to be quite productive because one day, the crying stopped. *Just like that.* I gathered my thoughts and recipe scraps, and my blog, The Clever Carrot, was born. This creative outlet chronicled my journey toward a more balanced lifestyle.

Growing up, I was surrounded by a strong European influence. My grandmother (on my mother's side) was French and worked in a family owned bistro in Paris. Everything was homemade: soups, stocks, braises—you name it. My grandmother (on my father's side) was Sicilian and created the most delicious and thoughtful meals on a tight budget. She wouldn't be caught dead with a bottle of jarred tomato sauce.

But nowadays, how do you fit homemade cooking into a modern schedule? We're all so busy being busy, we tend to gravitate toward quick and easy solutions (cereal, anyone?). Of course, takeout is a more popular option and who doesn't secretly wish to outsource cooking and cleaning to somebody else?

The premise of this book is to share my get-ahead strategies and time-saving tips for stress-free home cooking. More and more of us want to get back to basics, connect with our food and make it ourselves. We just need a way to get there. So I've applied my formal culinary training where it counts most, real life.

For example, cook one batch of my Triple-Duty Chicken Stock (page 27) and you'll have easy meal ideas for the rest of the week. Learn how to make authentic takeout-style dishes using my simple Master Stir-Fry Sauce (page 51). I'll even share my secrets for the best Banana Cloud Cake (page 142) you'll ever sink your teeth into.

My approach is not a gimmick, rather an alternate route that empowers the home cook and squashes the stigma associated with cooking from scratch. We could all use more time; it's about using your time *wisely*. This book is for everyone. Flip through the pages and be inspired. Pick what works best for you. With a little clever planning—and most of all, with confidence—you'll be one step closer to owning your time in the kitchen.

Because at the end of the day, we all have to eat!

xo Emilie

*chapter one*

# PREP-AHEAD VEGETABLES

Imagine this: You're about to run out the door, you're running late and you have just enough time to throw something in the slow cooker. Suddenly, you remember a container of veggies prepped earlier in the week... into the pot it goes! Upon your return, a delicious, homemade dinner is ready and you barely lifted a finger... not even to peel a carrot.

Sign. Me. Up.

When doing research for this book, I hung out at the grocery store, *a lot*. And it was not just to buy food. I would grab a coffee and a blueberry muffin and wander around the store peeking into everyone's cart. What were they shopping for?

Nowadays, you can buy all kinds of convenience items: stir-fry vegetables, peeled garlic, shredded coleslaw—the list goes on. The most popular item? Chopped vegetables. Regardless of freshness or price, containers of onions, carrots and celery flew off the shelves.

In this chapter, you'll learn how to prep and store your own chopped vegetables with delicious recipes to go along with them. This is one of the most useful get-ahead strategies in the book. Your time upfront significantly cuts down on future prep time and eliminates the temptation for overpriced, store-bought items. Trust me, I have two beautiful little boys who cling to my body like squid and this trick is *brilliant for* when you're short on time (or free hands).

# PRE-CHOPPED VEGETABLES (MIREPOIX)

GLUTEN-FREE — VEGETARIAN — VEGAN

Pronounced "mir-pwah," it's the classic French term for the combination of diced onions, carrots and celery. This powerhouse trio adds great flavor to soups, stews, stocks and braised dishes. If you think about it, most recipes will contain at least one of the three vegetables. Having a stash of mirepoix used together or separately works wonders for quick "prep-less" meals.

### YIELDS 2 QUARTS (850 G) DICED ONION, ¼ QUART (365 G) DICED CARROTS, 1 QUART (455 G) DICED CELERY

2 lbs (907 g) yellow onions

1 lb (454 g) bunch of carrots

1 lb (454 g) bunch of celery

NOTE: Due to their high water content, frozen vegetables tend to lose their shape when defrosted. They are best used in sauces, soups, stocks and slow cooker meals.

TIP:
1 medium onion = 1 cup (160 g) diced
1 medium carrot = ½ cup (65 g) diced
1 medium celery stalk = ½ cup (50 g) diced

To create your own arsenal of mirepoix, you have two options:

» Chop your vegetables by hand.
» Get yourself one of those inexpensive handheld choppers for quick, precise dicing.

*I highly recommend the latter.* The chopper I use features a grid-shaped dicing blade and storage container underneath (see picture). Simply place your vegetables on top of the blade, close the lid and push down; in a matter of seconds you'll end up with perfectly diced vegetables. Even if you don't mind chopping a carrot here and there, this shortcut makes prep work faster, easier and less stressful—it's worth it for the onions alone! Usually, I'll distract the kids with an art activity and join them at the table with my vegetables. They color, while I chop. Plus, I might even get them to eat a vegetable or two....

Vary the quantities listed above based on what you use most. For example, I go through onions quickly during the week, so I prep extra to freeze. Celery? Not so much.

Start by washing, trimming and peeling all vegetables, as needed.

### TO SLICE BY HAND
Cut into ½-inch (1.3-cm) dice.

### TO USE A HANDHELD CHOPPER
Slice the onions in half and place on the dicing blade, one half at a time. Close the lid and press down to dice. Empty the storage container for the next vegetable. Quarter the carrots, and arrange comfortably to fit on the blade. Dice the carrots, and then empty the container. Repeat for the celery stalks.

For storage, place each vegetable in separate airtight containers, draping a damp paper towel over the top. This will preserve freshness. Label and date your veggies. Refrigerate up to 1 week. Alternatively, each vegetable can be frozen separately, 1–3 months.

# SPRING TORTELLINI MINESTRONE

Italian minestrone is the ultimate comfort food. This version is light and simple, inspired by the first baby greens of spring. My local Italian deli makes the most wonderful pillowy-soft tortellini and I like to combine them with Pre-Chopped Vegetables (page 11) for quick soups and pasta dinners.

## SERVES 6

1 tbsp (15 ml) olive oil

1 tbsp (15 g) unsalted butter

½ cup (80 g) diced onions

½ cup (65 g) diced carrots

½ cup (50 g) diced celery

Coarse salt and freshly ground black pepper

1 clove of garlic, grated

1 tbsp (16 g) tomato paste

1 (14-oz [397-g]) can of diced tomatoes

1 quart (1 L) of Triple-Duty Chicken Stock (page 27)

1 (9-oz [255-g]) package cheese tortellini

1 cup (135 g) fresh or frozen peas

2–3 large handfuls of baby spinach, kale or other spring greens

¼ cup (6 g) fresh basil leaves

Wedge of Parmesan cheese, for grating

In a large, heavy-bottom pot, melt the olive oil and butter over medium heat. Sauté the onions, carrots and celery until soft and lightly golden, about 5–7 minutes. Season with salt and pepper. Add the garlic and tomato paste. Stir well until the tomato paste is fully dissolved and the garlic is fragrant, about 30 seconds.

Pour in the diced tomatoes and chicken stock. Place the lid on top and bring the soup to a gentle boil. Reduce the heat to low and simmer (lid tilted) for about 10 minutes, stirring occasionally. Continue to cook until the vegetables are tender.

Right before serving, increase the heat and bring the soup back to a gentle boil to cook the pasta. Add the tortellini, peas and greens. Simmer, uncovered for just about 3 minutes. Remove the pot from the heat; the tortellini will continue to cook without absorbing all of the broth.

Stack the basil leaves on top of each other, roll them up and cut across into ribbons.

Ladle your soup into bowls and dust with a generous grating of Parmesan cheese. Sprinkle with the basil ribbons. Once the herbs touch down onto the hot soup, you will be hit with the most wonderful aroma....

VARIATION #1: SWEET ITALIAN SAUSAGE: Squeeze the meat from its casing (about 1 pound [454 g] should be good) and sauté with the vegetables. The fennel from the sausage adds great flavor to the broth.

VARIATION #2: VEGETARIAN: Add 1 teaspoon of fennel seeds instead, and substitute with vegetable stock.

# EASY CHUNKY VEGETABLE SOUP

GLUTEN-FREE

When all else fails, and you *think* there's nothing to eat in your fridge, dig out whatever onions, carrots and celery you can find and make this easy vegetable soup. Having Pre-Chopped Vegetables (page 11) will cut down on prep, but if you don't have any on hand, you can still whip this up in a reasonable amount of time (especially with one of those handheld choppers I raved about earlier!).

Curling up with a quick, homemade soup that's simple and good for you is a lifesaver during a busy week.

SERVES 4

1 tbsp (15 ml) olive oil

1 tbsp (15 g) unsalted butter

1 cup (160 g) diced onions

1 cup (130 g) diced carrots

1 cup (100 g) diced celery

Coarse salt and freshly ground black pepper

3 cups (450 g) diced Yukon Gold potatoes, skin on (about 2 medium potatoes)

4 cups (946 ml) Triple-Duty Chicken Stock (page 27), plus more as needed

2 tbsp (8 g) roughly chopped parsley

In a large, heavy-bottom pot, warm the olive oil and butter over medium-low heat. Add the onions, carrots and celery and sauté until soft, about 5–7 minutes. Season with salt and pepper.

Add the potatoes. Pour the stock over the vegetables. Place the lid on top and bring the soup to a gentle boil. Reduce the heat to low and simmer (lid tilted) until the vegetables are tender, about 20–30 minutes.

Working in batches, carefully purée the soup to a chunky-smooth consistency. You can do this using a hand blender, food processor or regular blender. (Always use caution when blending hot liquids; wait until slightly cooled if necessary.) Add additional stock as needed to get the texture to your liking.

To the pot, sprinkle in the chopped parsley. Stir well. Taste and adjust seasoning as needed.

To serve, ladle the hot soup into bowls and enjoy.

TIP: If you're in the mood, try adding a generous dusting of curry spice, spicy chili flakes or coconut milk to diversify the flavors. Woodsy herbs such as thyme, sage and rosemary are nice too. Substitute with vegetable stock as needed.

# 30-MINUTE BROCCOLI & FETA SOUP

GLUTEN-FREE

This soup was originally destined for a block of sharp cheddar until I realized, at the last minute, that my husband had used the last bit of cheese to make a quesadilla...for me! Go figure. On a whim, I used feta instead. Combined with onions and celery from my stash of Pre-Chopped Vegetables (page 11), this soup came together quickly, about 30 minutes or so, and was unexpectedly delicious. The feta adds a touch of subtle creaminess and does not overpower the natural sweetness of the broccoli.

PS: The secret to bright green soup is to briefly cook the broccoli and purée with a generous handful of parsley.

## SERVES 4–6

2 tbsp (30 ml) olive oil

1 cup (160 g) diced onions

½ cup (50 g) diced celery

2 garlic cloves, smashed

Coarse salt and freshly ground black pepper

1 large Yukon Gold potato, skin on, about 1½ cups (225 g) diced

4 cups (946 ml) Triple-Duty Chicken Stock (page 27), plus more as needed

6 cups (546 g) broccoli florets

⅓ cup (20 g) parsley leaves

⅓ cup (50 g) feta cheese

### TOPPINGS

Extra feta crumbles

Handful of parsley leaves

Drizzle of olive oil

In a large, heavy-bottom pot, warm the olive oil over medium heat. Sauté the onions, celery and smashed garlic cloves until soft, about 5–7 minutes. Season with salt and pepper. Add the potatoes and give it a quick stir.

Pour in the stock. Place the lid on top and bring the soup to a gentle boil. Reduce the heat to low and simmer (lid tilted) for about 10–15 minutes or until the potatoes are soft.

Add the broccoli and cook briefly, about 3–4 minutes. Quick Tip: Be careful not to overcook the broccoli at this stage; the soup will turn yellowish-green (in terms of flavor it's not the end of the world; it just might look like swamp water).

Working in batches, carefully purée the soup with the parsley leaves and feta. You can do this using a hand blender, food processor or regular blender. I like this soup rustic style, somewhere in between smooth and chunky. But the texture is up to you. Add additional stock or water if necessary.

To serve, ladle the soup into bowls and sprinkle with extra feta crumbles, parsley leaves and a drizzle of olive oil.

TIP: Try adding a sprinkle of fresh dill (when available) for extra flavor. Substitute with vegetable stock or water as needed.

# SIMPLE BRAISED BEEF WITH PASTA

Traditionally, browning beef in a hot pan prior to braising is a classic cooking technique; it seals the meat and locks in flavor. But for time's sake, who needs rules? I've eliminated this step with surprisingly excellent results. Plus, I'm using a large 3-pound to 4-pound (1.4–1.8-kg) chuck roast, which can be cumbersome to sear in the first place. Combine the beef with Pre-Chopped Vegetables (page 11) in your slow cooker, hit the button and you're done. After six to eight hours of hands-off cooking, the beef will become incredibly tender, flavorful and melt-in-your-mouth delicious.

SERVES 4–6

3–4-lb (1.4–1.8-kg) whole beef chuck roast

Coarse salt and freshly ground black pepper

1 cup (160 g) diced onions

½ cup (65 g) diced carrots

½ cup (50 g) diced celery

3 garlic cloves, smashed

1 tbsp (15 ml) olive oil (optional), plus more for drizzling

1 (28-oz [794-g]) can of whole plum tomatoes in thick purée

¼ cup (65 g) tomato paste

1 lb (454 g) pappardelle pasta

Wedge of Parmesan cheese, for grating

TIP: For best quality, purchase a whole cut of boneless beef chuck instead of cubed "stewing beef." Whole cuts have better marbling, which refers to the pattern of fat lines that run throughout the meat. You'll get more flavor and tenderness with quality marbling.

Pat the beef dry with a paper towel to remove any excess moisture. Season all sides with salt and pepper.

Add the onions, carrots, celery and garlic to a 6-quart (6-L) slow cooker. Quick Tip: If you have time, sauté the vegetables in 1 tablespoon (15 ml) of olive oil before adding to the slow cooker (otherwise, throw them in raw).

Place the beef on top of the vegetables. Pour in the canned tomatoes and tomato paste.

Cook on low for 6–8 hours, checking on the beef at the 6-hour mark. You'll know it's ready when the meat is fall-apart tender, and shreds easily with a fork. Transfer to a cutting board and tent with foil to rest, about 10 minutes.

Pour the tomato braising liquid from the slow cooker into a large, 12-inch (30-cm) skillet. This is your sauce for the pasta. Adjust the heat to low, and skim away any fat that rises to the top. Season with salt and pepper to taste.

For the pasta, bring a pot of water to a boil and cook according to the package instructions. Drain and set aside. Drizzle with olive oil to prevent sticking.

Using two forks (or your hands), shred the beef into bite-size pieces. Sample a few pieces as you go—it's so tender! Add the beef to the sauce and stir gently to combine.

To serve, ladle your delicious slow-cooked beef over the pasta and sprinkle with freshly grated Parmesan cheese.

# BRAISED CHICKEN WITH RED WINE & MUSHROOMS

My French grandmother's classic coq au vin was to die for. She cooked it in an electric skillet, *outside*. You could smell the tantalizing aroma of red wine and garlic wafting throughout the entire neighborhood. My mom said this was why all the kids used to play at her house. Luckily, I inherited that electric skillet. But rather than babysitting (and sweating) over a hot pan, I've minimized the prep to make this recipe come together quickly: Simply sauté the bacon and chicken respectively, and then throw everything into the slow cooker with Pre-Chopped Vegetables (page 11). Serve with quick creamy polenta for the ultimate winter warmer.

SERVES 4–6

½ cup (63 g) flour

6–8 chicken thighs, bone-in, skinless

Coarse salt and freshly ground black pepper

1 tsp olive oil, plus more as needed

4 slices of bacon, cut into ½-inch (1.3-cm) pieces

1 cup (160 g) diced onion

½ cup (65 g) diced carrot

½ cup (50 g) diced celery

2 garlic cloves, smashed

4–6 sprigs of thyme

1 (10-oz [283-g]) box of baby portobello mushrooms

1 cup (237 ml) dry red wine

1 cup (237 ml) Triple-Duty Chicken Stock (page 27)

2 tbsp (8 g) roughly chopped parsley

QUICK CREAMY POLENTA

4 cups (946 ml) milk

Coarse salt

1 cup (160 g) instant polenta

1 tbsp (15 g) unsalted butter

Freshly ground pepper

To begin, add the flour to a large zip-top bag. Season the chicken with salt and pepper. Add the chicken to the bag and shake well to coat.

In a large, 12-inch (30-cm) skillet, warm the olive oil over medium-low heat. Cook the bacon until golden, about 5 minutes. Transfer to a paper towel–lined plate and set aside. Keep the drippings in the pan.

Place the chicken (meaty side down) in the skillet, shaking off any excess flour as you go. Brown the meat, about 2–3 minutes per side. Add more olive oil as needed.

To a 6-quart (6-L) slow cooker, add the onions, carrots, celery, garlic and thyme (see tip below for alternate cooking method). Using your hands, tear up the mushrooms and drop them directly into the pot; this method is much faster than slicing and adds great texture to the dish. Pour in the wine and chicken stock. Cook on high for about 3–4 hours or on low for 6 hours. Your chicken is ready when the meat is falling off the bone. Taste the sauce and season with salt and pepper.

About 30 minutes prior to serving, start your polenta. In a medium-size saucepan, bring the milk and a pinch of salt to a boil. Cook according to the package instructions. Remove the pot from the heat and add the butter. Season with salt and pepper. Keep covered until ready to use.

Portion the polenta into shallow bowls and top with your braised chicken. Sprinkle with the reserved bacon and chopped parsley. Don't forget to take in the aroma before diving in—it will smell wonderful.

TIP: As an alternate cooking method, after browning chicken, add the ingredients to a large Dutch oven and braise at 350°F (177°C) for about 1½ hours or until tender.

# WEEKNIGHT PASTA WITH MEAT SAUCE

It was winter. We had just returned home from a relaxing, tropical family vacation only to find no food in the house. *What a nightmare!* Two seconds away from a frantic low-blood-sugar meltdown, I unearthed the contents of the freezer. And there it was...a bag of Pre-Chopped Vegetables (page 11). Knowing I could whip up a quick meat sauce without having to chop a single onion, carrot or celery took the edge off, considerably. Nothing like familiar comfort food, fast.

SERVES 4

1 lb (454 g) pasta, such as shells

2 tbsp (30 g) unsalted butter

1 tbsp (15 ml) olive oil

2 cups (320 g) diced onion

½ cup (65 g) diced carrots

½ cup (50 g) diced celery

2 cloves of garlic, grated

1 tsp fennel seeds

½ lb (227 g) ground beef

½ lb (227 g) ground pork

Coarse salt and freshly ground black pepper

¼ cup (65 g) tomato paste

1 (28-oz [794-g]) can whole-peeled plum tomatoes in thick purée

Wedge of Parmesan cheese, for grating

Handful of fresh basil leaves (optional)

Bring a pot of water to a boil and cook the pasta according to the package instructions. Drain and return back to the pot. Add the butter and stir well to prevent sticking.

Meanwhile, in a large pot, warm the olive oil over low heat. Sauté the onions, carrots, celery and garlic until lightly golden, about 5-7 minutes. Add the fennel seeds. Quick Tip: Alternatively, blitz the vegetables in the food processor to break them down into a "pulp." They will cook faster this way and the vegetables will blend seamlessly into the sauce.

Add the ground beef and ground pork. Brown the meat for about 5 minutes or so, stirring occasionally with a wooden spoon to break up the meat. Season with salt and pepper. If there is liquid in the pan continue to cook gently—no need to boil rapidly—until the moisture has evaporated.

Add the tomato paste and stir to dissolve. Pour in the canned tomatoes.

Bring the sauce to a rolling boil. Reduce the heat to low and simmer (uncovered) for about 25-30 minutes. The meat should be cooked through and the tomatoes slightly thickened. Give it a taste and season with extra salt and pepper, if necessary.

To serve, mix 1-2 ladles of meat sauce with the pasta to coat. Portion into bowls with extra sauce on top. Sprinkle with Parmesan cheese and basil leaves, if using.

TIP: Freeze this meat sauce in containers to defrost for quick weeknight dinners, up to 3 months.

*chapter two*

# BACK TO BASICS

There are certain things I can't live without.

Chocolate? Must have. Toothpaste? Non-negotiable. Cell phone? Obviously. The same rules apply in my kitchen, only they manifest themselves in the form of homemade culinary shortcuts.

This section is broken down into three parts: Triple-Duty Chicken Stock (page 27), Basic Tomato Sauce (page 40) and Master Stir-Fry Sauce (page 51). These are my go-to, prep-ahead basics.

When you have these essentials on hand, it's like having premium gas in your car; you can go anywhere. Not only that, I've come up with faster ways to make them, leaving you free as a bird to attend to more serious matters, such as folding laundry or finding the lids to your Tupperware....

Whatever recipes you choose in this chapter, the idea is to use your time wisely to make life easier in the kitchen. When you sit down to a wholesome, home-cooked meal, you will feel accomplished without wanting to take a nap!

# TRIPLE-DUTY CHICKEN STOCK

GLUTEN-FREE

Yes, I know what you're thinking... Homemade stock? Who has time for that?! Here's the deal: Homemade stock is the foundation for flavorful, homemade cooking. There's no question. And I've come up with a strategy to make this method pay off, or else I wouldn't do it myself.

By using a whole chicken, this stock only needs about 1½ hours to cook. Any longer and the breast meat will begin to dry out. Your reward? A gorgeous pot of liquid gold for soups and risottos, and a whole chicken that will yield several meals. And if you're really clever, you can easily reuse the bones to make another batch of stock (see tip). Homemade chicken stock is a triple-duty reward, making planning and cooking meals one less thing you have to worry about. It's good for the soul too.

## MAKES ABOUT 2½ QUARTS (2½ L)

1 whole chicken, about 4–5 lbs (1.8–2.3 kg)

2 cups (320 g) diced onion

1 cup (130 g) diced carrots

1 cup (100 g) diced celery

1 heaped tbsp (6.5 g) fennel seeds

2 tsp (10 g) black peppercorns

1 bunch of parsley stems

2 bay leaves

10 thyme sprigs

12 cups (3 L) water

TIP: Don't throw away those bones! Freeze leftover bones from previous stock and roast chicken dinners to make another batch of homemade stock. Follow the recipe here, increasing the cooking time to about 8 hours. Cooking the bones for a longer period of time makes a nutritious broth full of vitamins and minerals. It's perfect for the slow cooker.

Place all of the ingredients into a large, 6-quart (6-L) pot. Cover with water. Bring the stock to a gentle boil and reduce the heat to low. Simmer (lid tilted) for about 1½ hours, or until the chicken is cooked through. Skim away any foam that floats to the top.

Place the chicken in a large bowl, breast side down. Cover with 2 cups (475 ml) of stock. Quick Tip: Whenever you slow-cook or braise, it's important to let the meat rest in some of its cooking liquid so that it doesn't dry out. Placing the chicken breast side down will keep the meat juicy.

Grab a large strainer and drape a clean kitchen towel inside. Strain the stock over a large bowl, using a ladle to push down on the vegetables to extract the liquid. Discard the vegetables when you're done. Cool the stock (and meat) to room temperature before storing. Don't forget to add back the 2 cups (475 ml) of stock from the chicken.

Pour the strained stock into airtight containers or zip-top bags. Divide it into small portions for convenience. Label and date accordingly. Refrigerate for about 1 week, or freeze up to 6 months.

For the chicken, shred the meat using two forks (or your hands). Feel free to mix the white and dark meat together or store separately, depending on your preference. Portion into containers or zip-top bags for quick dinners. The chicken will keep in the fridge 3–4 days and in the freezer, up to 3 months.

(continued)

NOTES:

»  Pre-Chopped Vegetables (page 11) are perfect for stock. Chopped vegetables (as opposed to whole carrots, celery and onions) add more flavor.

»  Parsley stems add great flavor to stock. The next time you have a bunch of fresh parsley, slice off the stems and freeze. Fresh parsley is best; dried parsley and other herbs can be quite strong.

»  Purchase the best quality chicken you can afford. To really benefit from the nutrients of homemade stock, it is essential to use the good stuff; go organic and/or free-range.

»  Don't be afraid of gelatin. If your stock looks wobbly after you take it out of the fridge—this is normal; it's the natural gelatin setting up. The stock will return to its liquid state once heated.

»  Keep your chicken stock versatile. Don't go crazy adding salt and seasonings, build as you go.

»  For vegetable stock, double the amount of vegetables and omit the chicken. Then follow the recipe as usual.

# EASY CONCENTRATED STOCK CUBES

GLUTEN-FREE

My freezer is a war zone. You need a helmet and an ice pick to excavate that thing; it's filled to the brim! Concentrated stock cubes are not only convenient, they barely take up any space. Simply reduce one batch of Triple-Duty Chicken Stock (page 27) to about 1½ cups (355 ml). Watch it carefully, though, it will cook down faster than you think. Pour into ice cube trays, chill and freeze.

## MAKES ENOUGH CUBES FOR 2½ QUARTS (2½ L) STOCK

1 batch of Triple-Duty Chicken Stock (page 27), about 2½ quarts [2½ L]

TIP: To reconstitute, 1 frozen stock cube + 1 cup (237 ml) of water = 1 cup (237 ml) of chicken stock.

Pour your chicken stock into a large soup pot. Bring to a rolling boil, then reduce the heat to low. Simmer (uncovered) for about 45 minutes to 1 hour. You should have about 1½ cups (355 ml). As it cooks, skim away any foam that floats to the top. This will make your stock cubes clear, not cloudy.

Cool down to room temperature, about 10 minutes, before storing.

Pour your cooled stock into ice cube trays for easy storage. Freeze until solid. Once frozen, transfer to a large zip-top bag or container, and label and date accordingly. Stock cubes should last up to 6 months.

# SPEEDY CHICKEN SOUP

One of the many benefits of Triple-Duty Chicken Stock (page 27) is chicken soup on demand. Simmer Pre-Chopped Vegetables (page 11) with pasta and leftover chicken. Right before serving, toss in heaping handfuls of tender baby greens to wilt. Dinner is on the table in under 30 minutes.

SERVES 4

1 tbsp (15 ml) olive oil

1 cup (130 g) diced carrots

1 cup (100 g) diced celery

2 quarts (2 L) Triple-Duty Chicken Stock (page 27), plus more as needed

½ cup (50 g) small tube pasta

4 cups (500 g) cooked shredded chicken

Coarse salt and freshly ground black pepper

4 large handfuls of baby greens, such as spinach or kale

Ground Parmesan cheese, to taste

In a large pot, heat the olive oil over low heat. Add the carrots and celery, and sauté until soft but not colored, about 3 minutes.

Pour in the chicken stock and bring the soup to a boil. Add the pasta and cook (uncovered) until al dente, about 7 minutes for small tube pasta. If using a different pasta variety, refer to the package for specific cooking time.

Reduce the heat to low, and add your shredded chicken. Simmer for about 5–6 minutes for the flavors to infuse and the chicken to soften. Season with salt and pepper. Right before serving, add your baby greens and stir gently to wilt.

Portion into bowls and sprinkle with lots of Parmesan cheese to taste.

# NO-STIR RISOTTO

**GLUTEN-FREE**

Gone are the days of stirring risotto! This recipe has bailed me out many times during a busy week—it's easy comfort food. Instead of being held prisoner by the wooden spoon, the convenience here is baking in the oven. Now you're free to do other things such as chase after small children running around the house naked.

Make sure to use arborio rice, which is classic for any type of risotto. Its natural starches release into the stock, making the risotto extra creamy and luxurious. This needs nothing more than a handful of your favorite seasonal greens and a good dusting of Parmesan cheese.

SERVES 4–6

1 tbsp (15 ml) olive oil

2 tbsp (30 g) unsalted butter, divided

1 cup (160 g) diced onions

¼ cup (25 g) diced celery

4½ cups (950 g) arborio rice

Splash of dry white vermouth

5 cups (1.2 L) Triple-Duty Chicken Stock (page 27), plus more as needed

Coarse salt and freshly ground black pepper

Wedge of Parmesan cheese, for grating

4 small handfuls of seasonal greens or herbs, such as pea shoots, basil or parsley

Preheat your oven to 350°F (175°C).

In a large Dutch oven, warm the olive oil and 1 tablespoon (15 g) of butter over medium heat. Sauté the onions and celery until soft, about 3–5 minutes. If the vegetables start to catch on the bottom of the pan lower the heat and add a splash of stock to slow down the cooking process.

Add the rice, and stir well to coat the grains. Toast the rice for about 1–2 minutes to intensify the flavor.

Pour in the vermouth. Continue to cook until the moisture has absorbed into the rice, 1–2 minutes. Feel free to pour yourself a glass while you're stirring! Add the chicken stock and season with salt and pepper.

Place the lid on top and pop it into the oven. Bake for about 45 minutes. When the risotto is ready, remove the lid and peek inside; it should look creamy and taste perfectly tender or al dente. Quick Tip: Classic risotto is not mushy. If yours is too thick, add more stock to get the texture nice and oozy. Risotto is forgiving.

To finish, stir in the remaining 1 tablespoon (15 g) of butter and grate some Parmesan cheese directly into the pot—as much or as little as you'd like. Cover for about 5 minutes or so, to let it rest. This is just one of those "things" that makes risotto taste better.

Serve in shallow bowls topped with the greens and plenty of extra cheese.

# STRAWBERRY BALSAMIC CHICKEN SALAD WITH QUICK-CANDIED WALNUTS & GOAT CHEESE

GLUTEN-FREE

My son refuses to eat strawberries that look "weird." If they're not perfectly shaped or dark ruby red in color, he'll insist on eating another snack (but they're organic!). We have a wild strawberry patch in our backyard and after rejecting several perfectly okay berries, Dillon handed over his bowl with utter disappointment. I made salad.

Using leftover shredded chicken is not only quick and convenient, but makes this salad wonderfully substantial. The quick-candied walnuts, addicting on their own, can be swapped out for pecans or even cashews if you'd like. It's empowering to know what can be done with banished berries and humble leftovers.

SERVES 4

### QUICK-CANDIED WALNUTS

1 tbsp (15 g) unsalted butter

¼ cup (55 g) brown sugar

1 tbsp (15 ml) water

1 cup (100 g) walnut halves

Pinch of coarse salt, to taste

### BALSAMIC-DIJON JAM JAR DRESSING

1 tsp Dijon mustard

1 tbsp (15 ml) balsamic vinegar

¼ cup (60 ml) red wine vinegar

½ cup (118 ml) olive oil

Coarse salt and freshly ground black pepper

1 head of Bibb lettuce

2 cups (250 g) cooked shredded chicken

2 cups (330 g) sliced strawberries

½ cup (136 g) crumbled goat cheese

For the walnuts, line a rimmed baking sheet with parchment paper—you will need this for the candied walnuts to cool. In a small skillet, melt the butter, sugar and water over low heat. Bring the mixture to a gentle boil, and simmer to thoroughly dissolve the sugar, about 2–3 minutes. Add the walnuts, a pinch of salt and stir well to coat. Resist the urge to sneak a bite; the sugar is incredibly hot and you'll burn your tongue!

Transfer the walnuts to your lined baking sheet. Spread them out evenly to cool, about 5–10 minutes.

To prepare the dressing, add the first four ingredients to an empty jam jar. Season with salt and pepper. Screw the lid on tight and shake vigorously to blend.

For the salad, gently tear the lettuce leaves into bite-size pieces. Add to a large bowl. Add the chicken and sliced strawberries.

When you're ready to eat, lightly drizzle the salad with some of the dressing. Top with crumbled goat cheese and candied walnuts.

TIP: To get ahead, the candied walnuts and dressing can be made in advance. Store the walnuts in an airtight container up to 3 days (if you don't eat them all). The dressing will last in the fridge up to 2 weeks.

# ONE-POT CREAMY ORZO WITH ASPARAGUS

One night while making dinner, I made an interesting mistake: The pot I used to cook orzo was too small. As the pasta boiled and swelled, the liquid spilled all over the place creating a huge, sticky mess. The logical solution would've been to transfer everything to a larger pot. But the lack of water made the pasta *extra starchy*, taking on a creamy risotto-like texture. It was delicious. We ate it cacio e pepe style, buttered with black pepper and Parmesan cheese.

Later, I re-created my mistake (in a larger pot) with less liquid to achieve that gorgeous silky texture. To make it even easier, the asparagus is cooked together with the orzo—it's one less pan to clean.

## SERVES 4

1 tbsp (15 ml) olive oil

4 oz (115 g) diced pancetta, about ¼ inch (6 mm)

1 clove of garlic, grated

1½ cups (250 g) orzo pasta

1 quart (1 L) Triple-Duty Chicken Stock (page 27), plus more as needed

1 lb (454 g) bunch of medium asparagus

1 tbsp (15 g) unsalted butter

Wedge of Parmesan cheese, for grating

A few turns of freshly ground black pepper

TIP: This creamy orzo is excellent the next day, served at room temperature with a squeeze of lemon juice and a sprinkle of Parmesan cheese.

In a medium pot, warm the olive oil over medium-low heat. Sauté the pancetta until lightly golden, about 3–4 minutes. Add the garlic and orzo, and stir for about 30 seconds. The garlic should smell warm and nutty, and the pasta will be glistening from the oil.

Pour in the chicken stock and bring to a boil. Reduce the heat and simmer (lid tilted) for about 15 minutes. As the orzo absorbs the liquid, the texture will begin to thicken. Stir occasionally to prevent sticking.

Meanwhile, prepare the asparagus. Snap off the woody ends at the base of each stalk and discard; they are too tough to eat. Slice the asparagus on a diagonal about ½-inch (1.3-cm) thick to mimic the angular shape of the orzo.

When your pasta is at the 15-minute mark, add the asparagus to the pot. Continue to cook (uncovered) until the asparagus is tender, about 3–5 minutes depending on size.

At this point, the texture of your orzo should be creamy and silky, not too thick. Quick Tip: Because different brands of pasta absorb liquid at varied rates, add additional chicken stock to your orzo as needed.

Add the butter and some freshly grated Parmesan cheese. Season with a few turns of freshly ground black pepper—you should be good on the salt from the pancetta.

Portion into shallow bowls and top with extra cheese, if you'd like.

# WEEKNIGHT CHICKEN POTPIE

*Crispy, buttery, flaky puff pastry.* It's too labor intensive to make from scratch on a weeknight, involving a series of folds, turns and lengthy chilling time in the fridge. But it's too darn tasty to pass up! As an alternative, frozen all-butter puff pastry is just as good and widely available. You can purchase pre-rolled square sheets, that's what I use. Remember to defrost your dough at room temperature or in the fridge overnight *before* you get started.

Another time-saver is using leftover shredded chicken and Pre-Chopped Vegetables (page 11). Without these two shortcuts, tack on additional time to cook the chicken and to chop up the vegetables yourself.

## SERVES 4 HUNGRY PEOPLE

1 tbsp (15 ml) olive oil

2 tbsp (30 g) unsalted butter

1 cup (160 g) diced onions

1 cup (130 g) diced carrots

½ cup (50 g) diced celery

1 tsp roughly chopped sage leaves

3 tbsp (23 g) flour

1½ cups (355 ml) Triple-Duty Chicken Stock (page 27)

¼ cup (60 ml) half and half

2 cups (250 g) cooked shredded chicken

½ cup (67 g) frozen peas

Coarse salt and freshly ground black pepper

### FOR THE PUFF PASTRY

1 egg, lightly beaten

1 tsp water

1 sheet of all-butter puff pastry, defrosted

Whole sage leaves, for decoration

Preheat your oven to 400°F (204°C). Grab a deep pie pan or 9 x 13-inch (23 x 33-cm) baking dish.

In a large, 12-inch (30-cm) skillet, warm the olive oil and butter over medium heat. Sauté the onions, carrots, celery and chopped sage leaves until soft, about 3–5 minutes. Reduce the heat to low. Sprinkle the flour over the vegetables and stir well with a wooden spoon; it will start to clump. Pour in the chicken stock and half and half. Bring the mixture to a gentle boil and simmer until thickened, about 1–2 minutes.

Fold in the chicken and frozen peas. Season with salt and pepper. Pour the filling into your baking dish and cool for about 5 minutes before placing the puff pastry on top; you don't want the dough to melt. Quick Tip: Stop here if you are making this dish in advance. Wrap it up (without the dough) and refrigerate until ready to bake.

In a small bowl, mix the egg and water together. This is your egg wash.

Clear away all kitchen clutter. Roll out 1 sheet of puff pastry to fit the size of your baking dish. If using a pie pan, the dough should easily fit the pan without rolling. Place the dough on top of the filling, casually tucking in the sides as you go—it doesn't have to look perfect. Brush with egg wash and decorate with sage leaves. If you don't have a pastry brush, a folded paper towel will work too. Using a paring knife, make a few slits through the dough for the steam to escape while baking.

Bake for about 30–40 minutes. Your potpie is ready when the top is perfectly golden brown, the filling is hot and bubbly, and your whole house smells like a fancy bistro.

TIP: Potpie filling freezes very well. Double or triple this recipe and freeze up to 3 months. Be sure not to freeze previously frozen chicken (cooked or uncooked) to avoid unfriendly bacteria.

# BASIC TOMATO SAUCE

GLUTEN-FREE — VEGETARIAN

Sure, you can buy a jar of tomato sauce from the store. But making it yourself is quick, easy and tastes so much better. My version is ready in 20 minutes and it's virtually prep-free. The secret? Cooking the sauce in a wide skillet. The increased surface area reduces the sauce faster than a traditional deep pot. Basic tomato sauce is an excellent shortcut to have on hand for quick pasta dinners, pizzas, soups and more.

In terms of flavor, I do not add garlic or go crazy with herbs and spices; it's a light and delicate sauce. I do, however, add butter. My inspiration comes from chef Marcella Hazan. Butter mellows out the natural acidity of the tomatoes making the sauce silky and rich. In my opinion, it's the best thing that's ever happened to homemade tomato sauce. Try it!

## MAKES 1½ QUARTS (1.5 L)

4 tbsp (60 g) unsalted butter

½ cup (80 g) diced onion

2 (28-oz [794-g]) cans of whole peeled plum tomatoes in thick purée

1 handful of basil leaves, when in season

Coarse salt, to taste

1–2 tsp (5–10 g) sugar

In a large, 12-inch (30-cm) skillet, gently melt the butter over low heat. Add the onions and cook until soft, about 3 minutes.

Add to the tomatoes to the pan. If using fresh basil leaves, throw them in too. Bring the sauce to a rolling boil and reduce the heat. Simmer (uncovered) for about 20 minutes, breaking up the tomatoes with a wooden spoon.

Taste the sauce, and season with salt. Add the sugar to balance any tart, acidic flavors. Quick Tip: The tomato sauce we had growing up was on the sweeter side (in a good way) so I'm a 1½ teaspoons (6 g) kind of gal.

At this point, your tomato sauce is ready. For a smoother texture, purée the sauce with a hand blender directly in the pan.

When the sauce has cooled down completely, transfer to airtight containers or zip-top bags and label accordingly. Refrigerate 4–5 days or freeze up to 3 months.

# 30-MINUTE CREAMY TOMATO BASIL SOUP

Want delicious soup, fast? Add a few simple ingredients to your Basic Tomato Sauce (page 40), and you'll have a bowl of creamy tomato basil heaven in under 30 minutes. I use half and half to lighten the texture, and the amount of sugar needed will depend on the acidity of your tomatoes. Serve with crunchy, quick-skillet croutons or tuna melts if you're nostalgic like me. My husband loves this soup....

## SERVES 4

1 tbsp (15 ml) olive oil

1 tbsp (30 g) unsalted butter

2 cups (320 g) diced onion

1 garlic clove, sliced

5 cups (1.2 L) Basic Tomato Sauce (page 40)

2 cups (473 ml) Triple-Duty Chicken Stock (page 27)

Coarse salt and freshly ground black pepper

½ cup (118 ml) half and half or cream

1–2 tbsp (12–24 g) sugar

Handful of fresh basil leaves

### QUICK-SKILLET CROUTONS

2 slices of country bread, such as sourdough

1 tbsp (15 g) unsalted butter

Coarse salt and freshly ground black pepper

In a large pot, warm the olive oil and butter over medium heat. Sauté the onions and garlic until soft, about 3–5 minutes.

Add the tomato sauce and chicken stock to the pot. Bring to a gentle boil. Reduce the heat and simmer (lid tilted) for about 15 minutes for the flavors to develop. Season with salt and pepper to taste. When your onions are tender, it's time to purée the soup.

Meanwhile, for the croutons, cut the slices of country bread into cubes about 1 inch (2.5 cm) thick. Melt the butter over medium heat in a large nonstick skillet. Add the bread cubes. Stir constantly until golden brown and crisp, about 5–6 minutes. Season lightly with salt and pepper. Transfer to a bowl and set aside.

Working in batches, carefully purée the soup until smooth. You can do this using a hand blender, food processor or regular blender. Pour in the half and half (or cream) and stir well.

For the sugar, start by adding 1 tablespoon (12 g). Add more sugar as needed to balance out the acidity.

Ladle the hot soup into bowls and top with crunchy croutons. Scatter fresh basil leaves over the top, to serve.

TIP: Try topping this soup with thinly sliced scallions or fresh chive flowers.

# MARKET VEGETABLE BAKED ZITI

VEGETARIAN

No matter how you look at it, baked ziti requires a couple of steps; it's the nature of the recipe. The key to its success is how you organize your time. Roast the vegetables while the pasta is cooking, and for your Basic Tomato Sauce (page 40), don't bother warming it up—the residual heat from the pasta plus baking time in the oven will warm it through (and it's one less pot to clean). Once assembled, use the broiler to quickly melt the cheese. It's a delicious, comforting meal.

PS: You will need a roasting pan at least 13.5 x 11 inches (34 x 28 cm) or larger for the baked ziti.

SERVES 4–6

Small pat of unsalted butter, for coating the pan

1 lb (454 g) ziti pasta

¼ cup (60 ml) olive oil, divided

2 cups (180 g) broccoli florets

1 small zucchini, cut into 1-inch (2.5-cm) chunks

1 small yellow summer squash, cut into 1-inch (2.5-cm) chunks

1 cup (80 g) eggplant, skin on, cut into 1-inch (2.5-cm) chunks

Coarse salt and freshly ground black pepper

3 cups (710 ml) Basic Tomato Sauce (page 40)

1 cup (108 g) grated fontina cheese

½ cup (100 g) ground Parmesan cheese

1 ball of fresh mozzarella, sliced into rounds

Preheat your oven to 425°F (220°C). Line a rimmed baking sheet with parchment paper for your vegetables.

Lightly coat a large roasting pan with butter. This is for your baked ziti.

Bring a large pot of water to a boil and cook the pasta according to the package instructions. Drain and set aside. Drizzle with 2 tablespoons (30 ml) of olive oil to prevent sticking.

Meanwhile, add the broccoli, zucchini, summer squash and eggplant to your lined baking sheet. Drizzle with the remaining 2 tablespoons (30 ml) of olive oil and season with salt and pepper. Toss with your hands. Roast until tender, about 20 minutes.

To assemble the baked ziti, mix the pasta, roasted vegetables, tomato sauce and fontina cheese together—I do this directly in my roasting pan. Sprinkle with Parmesan cheese and arrange the sliced mozzarella on top.

Broil the pasta on low until the cheese is melted and bubbling, about 3–5 minutes. Check on it from time to time to make sure that it doesn't burn (you know how broilers are). Allow the pasta to set for about 5 minutes before slicing.

TIP: You can use any combination of vegetables you like for this recipe. It's flexible.

# QUICK THIN-CRUST TORTILLA PIZZAS

VEGETARIAN

Thin-crust pizza is my jam. Flour tortillas (regular or whole grain) make excellent thin crust pizza bases. Spread Basic Tomato Sauce (page 40) over the top with fresh mozzarella and Parmesan cheese, and in less than 10 minutes, a delicious, crispy pizza shall emerge from the oven. Sprinkle with a handful of fresh basil leaves, and dinner is served.

SERVES 4

1 tsp olive oil

4 small tortillas, regular or whole wheat

8 tbsp (120 ml) Basic Tomato Sauce (page 40)

1 ball of fresh mozzarella cheese

¼ cup (50 g) ground Parmesan cheese

Handful of regular or baby basil leaves

Preheat your oven to 425°F (220°C). Grab two rimmed baking sheets and place them in the oven to heat up.

Add the olive oil to a small bowl. Lightly brush both sides of the tortillas with oil—use a folded paper towel if you don't have a pastry brush. This makes the tortillas crispy when baked.

Spread 2 tablespoons (30 ml) of tomato sauce onto each tortilla, leaving a ½-inch (1.3-cm) border around the edge for your "crust." Use the back of a spoon to help guide you. Cut the mozzarella cheese into thin slices and top each pizza base. Sprinkle with Parmesan cheese.

Bake for about 7 minutes or until the pizza is crisp and the cheese is melted. Rotate your pans and swap racks for even browning.

When the pizza is ready, top with a generous handful of basil leaves. *Mangia!*

TIP: When it is in season, look for opal or purple basil. It tastes just like regular basil, perhaps a little stronger and is an absolute stunner. Available at farmers' markets, or you can grow your own during the summer.

# 20-MINUTE SKILLET-BAKED SHRIMP & FETA

Instead of serving crudités and dip at your next get together, try this easy one-pan skillet bake. In 15–20 minutes, you'll have blushing pink shrimp topped with chunky cubes of feta, slightly blackened from the broiler. Serve with thick slices of crusty bread. It's non-negotiable: One must use bread in lieu of utensils to eagerly scoop up the sauce.

## SERVES 6–8 AS AN APPETIZER, OR 4 AS A MAIN MEAL

1–1¼ lbs (450–570 g) peeled and deveined shrimp, tail on

Coarse salt and freshly ground black pepper

2 tbsp (30 ml) olive oil, divided

½ cup (80 g) diced onions

1 garlic clove, grated

1½ cups (355 ml) Basic Tomato Sauce (page 40)

½ cup (75 g) block feta, broken into large chunks

1 tsp dried oregano

Good crusty bread, for dunking

Adjust your oven racks to fit the top third portion of the oven. Preheat to 425°F (220°C).

Pat the shrimp dry with paper towels to remove any excess moisture. Season lightly with salt and pepper.

In a large, 10-inch (25-cm) oven-proof skillet, warm 1 tablespoon (15 ml) olive oil over medium heat. Sauté the onions until soft, about 3–5 minutes. Add the garlic and cook until fragrant, about 30 seconds.

Pour the tomato sauce into the pan. Add the shrimp. Arrange the feta over the top and sprinkle with dried oregano. Drizzle lightly with the remaining tablespoon (15 ml) of olive oil.

Bake on the top rack for about 15 minutes, or until the shrimp is cooked through. To quickly brown the feta, broil for a minute or so, but don't overdo it—you'll overcook the shrimp.

Serve directly in the skillet with thick slices of crusty bread.

TIP: If your shrimp are particularly large (or small), peek into the oven as they bake and adjust your cooking time accordingly.

# MASTER STIR-FRY SAUCE

### GLUTEN-FREE OPTION

Want to know a secret? According to my friend, whose family owns a fleet of Chinese restaurants, it's common to use only *one* master sauce for specialty Asian dishes. This makes cooking quick and streamlined. To diversify the flavor, various ingredients such as ginger, sesame oil, lemongrass, etc., are used to enhance the base sauce.

Adopting this shortcut in your own kitchen is easy; quickly whisk a few ingredients together and store in an empty jam jar. It takes 30 seconds. What I love most is that the classic salty-sweet proportions are premeasured, so there is no guesswork as to whether you have nailed that signature "takeout" flavor. Simply add to your favorite stir-fry and watch it become thick and glossy. This recipe can easily be doubled or tripled.

### MAKES 1½ CUPS (190 ML)

⅓ cup (78 ml) soy sauce (or tamari for gluten-free)

1 cup (237 ml) Triple-Duty Chicken Stock (page 27)

2 tbsp (30 ml) honey

3 tsp (8 g) cornstarch

Add all of the ingredients to a bowl. Whisk well for the honey and cornstarch to thoroughly dissolve. Pour into an empty jam jar and refrigerate up to 2 weeks.

To use, add your master sauce to any stir-fry, such as Quick Chicken Stir-Fry with Roasted Broccoli (page 52), and simmer until thickened.

> TIP: The cornstarch will eventually settle to the bottom of the jar over time. This is normal. Just give it a shake or a quick whisk before using.

# QUICK CHICKEN STIR-FRY WITH ROASTED BROCCOLI

GLUTEN-FREE OPTION

I make a stir-fry at least once a week. It's quick, straightforward and flexible. But here's what I've learned: If you overcrowd the pan with too many ingredients (which I tend to do) your stir-fry will steam and become watery rather than thicken and caramelize. I solve this dilemma by multitasking—roast the bulky broccoli in the oven while making the rest of the dish on the stove. The broccoli becomes nutty and sweet and goes well with the rich flavors of honey and soy.

SERVES 2

1 head of broccoli

4 tbsp (60 ml) vegetable oil, divided

2 boneless, skinless chicken breasts, thinly sliced

2 cloves of garlic, grated

1 cup (237 ml) Master Stir-Fry Sauce (page 51)

2 scallions, thinly sliced, white and light green parts only

Preheat your oven to 425°F (220°C). Line a rimmed baking sheet with parchment paper.

Cut the broccoli into bite-size florets—you want them roughly the same size. Add the broccoli to your baking sheet and drizzle with 2 tablespoons (30 ml) of vegetable oil and toss with your hands. Roast in the oven for about 15–20 minutes, giving it a stir after 10 minutes or so. The broccoli should look golden brown.

Meanwhile, in a wok or a large, 10-inch (25-cm) cast-iron skillet, heat the remaining 2 tablespoons (30 ml) of vegetable oil over medium-high heat. When the pan is hot, add the chicken and sauté for about 2–3 minutes. Add the garlic and stir until fragrant, 30 seconds.

Quick Tip: Before adding the stir-fry sauce to the pan, give it a quick shake or whisk to dissolve any cornstarch that has settled to the bottom. Otherwise, the sauce won't thicken properly.

Pour the stir-fry sauce into the pan. Bring the mixture to a boil, and then simmer for 1–2 minutes to thicken the sauce.

Once the sauce is nice and glossy and the chicken is cooked through, remove the pan from the heat.

To serve, pile the chicken and broccoli into shallow bowls. Sprinkle with scallions.

TIP: No wok? No problem! Use a hot cast-iron skillet for any stir-fry recipe to achieve a charred, smoky flavor.

# A HEALTHIER SWEET & SOUR PORK

GLUTEN-FREE

If you're looking for neon red sauce, this isn't it. If you're looking for nuggets of deep-fried pork, this isn't that either. My version of the classic Chinese takeout dish is made healthier, with sautéed juicy pork tenderloin fortified with the clean flavors of balsamic vinegar and honey. This is a perfect example of how to easily transform your Master Stir-Fry Sauce (page 51) with just a few simple ingredients.

Beware: There is cilantro in this dish. I happen to think the combination of pineapple and cilantro is superb; however, I recognize that the mere mention of the word cilantro can be polarizing. Leave it out if you think I'm crazy.

SERVES 4

1 lb (454 g) pork tenderloin, trimmed

1 cup (237 ml) Master Stir-Fry Sauce (page 51)

1 tbsp (15 ml) balsamic vinegar

¼ cup (60 ml) ketchup

¼ cup (85 g) honey

1 tbsp (15 ml) vegetable oil

1 clove of garlic, grated

1 (2-inch [5-cm]) piece of ginger, peeled and grated

1 red bell pepper, cut into strips

1 heaping cup (165 g) of pineapple, cut into bite-size pieces

Fresh cilantro or parsley leaves (optional)

Brown rice, for serving (optional)

Thinly slice the pork tenderloin into ¼-inch to ½-inch (6–13-mm) rounds.

For the sweet and sour sauce, add your Master Stir-Fry Sauce (shake it up first), balsamic vinegar, ketchup and honey to a large bowl. Whisk well to dissolve.

In a large, 10-inch (25-cm) cast-iron skillet, warm the vegetable oil over medium heat. Add the pork, and sear about 2–3 minutes. Work in batches to avoid overcrowding the pan. Set the pork aside.

Add the garlic, ginger and red bell pepper. Sauté for about 2–3 minutes to soften the peppers. Quick Tip: Before adding your sweet and sour sauce, give it a quick whisk to redistribute the ingredients.

Pour the sweet and sour sauce into the pan. Bring the mixture to a boil, and simmer for 1–2 minutes to thicken the sauce. Add the pork back along with the pineapple. Cook for about 1 minute to allow the flavors to mingle.

Add your sweet and sour pork to a large serving bowl. Scatter with optional cilantro (or parsley) leaves. Serve with brown rice, if desired.

TIP: You are more than welcome to use fresh, frozen or canned pineapple. If using frozen pineapple, thaw slightly before adding to the sauce. For canned pineapple, drain the juice and use the fruit only—if you add all of the juice it will get too watery, although 1 or 2 tablespoons (15–30 ml) for extra pineapple flavor wouldn't hurt.

# 30-MINUTE ASIAN CHICKEN LETTUCE WRAPS

GLUTEN-FREE OPTION

Memories of good meals stay with me forever. In college, I lived with a fantastic cook who loved to entertain. One night Christine hosted a fun girls' get-together featuring a simple yet impressive menu: Asian chicken lettuce wraps with homemade chocolate fudge cake for dessert! Although this is not Christine's original recipe, it was inspired by her memorable feast.

Lettuce wraps are not only great for entertaining, they present themselves as a quick weeknight meal option. For this particular version, nutty sesame oil is added to diversify the Master Stir-Fry Sauce (page 51). Sliced apple, perhaps an unusual addition, provides a refreshing crunch against the zesty ginger.

## SERVES 4

1 head of Bibb or Iceberg lettuce

¼ tsp sesame oil

1 tbsp (15 ml) vegetable oil

1 lb (454 g) ground chicken or turkey, white and dark meat mix for best flavor

2 cloves of garlic, grated

1 (2-inch [5-cm]) piece of fresh ginger, peeled and grated

1 cup (237 ml) Master Stir-Fry Sauce (page 51)

1 green apple, skin on

1 tbsp (10 g) sesame seeds

Place the Bibb (or Iceberg) lettuce on its side and slice off about ½ inch (1.3 cm) at the base; the leaves will separate easier this way. Wash and dry the leaves and set aside until ready to use.

Warm the sesame oil and vegetable oil in a large, 10-inch (25-cm) cast-iron skillet. Add the ground chicken (or turkey). Cook until lightly browned, about 4–5 minutes, or until all of the moisture has evaporated. Add the garlic and ginger, and stir until fragrant, about 30 seconds. Quick Tip: Before adding the stir-fry sauce to the pan, give it a quick shake or whisk to dissolve any cornstarch that has settled to the bottom. Otherwise, the sauce won't thicken properly.

Pour the stir-fry sauce into the pan. Bring to a boil and simmer for 1–2 minutes to thicken. Remove the pan from the heat.

Cut your apple into thin slices and then across into thin, matchstick-size strips.

To assemble, add spoonfuls of your flavorful chicken filling to the crisp lettuce leaves. Top with a few apple sticks, sprinkle with sesame seeds and tuck in!

TIP: To get ahead, the filling can prepared up to 2 days in advance. Store in an airtight container in the fridge. To reheat, add the filling to a nonstick pan and gently warm through.

# QUICK-BRAISED BABY BOK CHOY

GLUTEN-FREE OPTION

When baby bok choy shows up in my CSA delivery box, I squeal with delight. To me, bok choy is one of the most tasty, albeit underused, vegetables around. It belongs to the cabbage family. Keep your eyes peeled for this versatile veg, the season runs from early summer to mid fall.

Generally speaking, "quick" and "braise" normally don't go together, as the latter refers to low and slow cooking. But because baby bok choy is so small and tender, this dish is a breeze to make.

## SERVES 4, AS A SIDE DISH

4 heads of baby bok choy

2 tbsp (30 ml) olive oil

1 clove of garlic, grated

¾ cup (177 ml) Master Stir-Fry Sauce (page 51)

¼ tsp red pepper flakes

Slice your baby bok choy in half lengthwise or into quarters if they're large. Give them a good rinse under cold water to remove any grit or sand caught in between the leaves. Dry thoroughly.

In a large, 12-inch (30-cm) skillet, warm the olive oil over medium heat. Once the pan is hot, add the bok choy, alternating placement base to leaves as you go. Cover and cook for about 3–4 minutes.

Remove the lid and flip the bok choy over. Continue to cook (uncovered) for another minute. To check for doneness, insert a small paring knife into the base; if it comes out easily, they're ready. If there's resistance, cook for another minute. Transfer to a serving platter.

Add the garlic to the pan and stir until fragrant, 30 seconds.

Quick Tip: Before adding the stir-fry sauce to the pan, give it a quick shake or whisk to dissolve any cornstarch that has settled to the bottom. Otherwise, the sauce won't thicken properly.

Pour the stir-fry sauce into the pan. Bring to a boil, and simmer for 1–2 minutes to thicken.

Spoon the glossy sauce over the bok choy and sprinkle with red pepper flakes.

*chapter three*

# COMPOUND BUTTERS

Sounds fancy, doesn't it?

By definition, compound or flavored butters are combined with different types of herbs and spices, citrus zest and sometimes sweetened with sugar. But this technique is not just for show, it's a brilliant shortcut. Use compound butters to effortlessly enhance the flavor of your recipes. Every time I open the fridge (or freezer) I'm inspired to experiment, whether it's quickly tossing a pat of garlic butter to create a simple pan sauce or mixing sweet cinnamon sugar butter into crumbles for dessert.

There are plenty of flavor combinations to play around with and subsequently, compound butters are a great way to use up odds and ends in the kitchen. But in this chapter we will keep it simple and stick to two classics that you are sure to use regularly once you try them. Whether wrapped up in a log or portioned into the perfect tablespoon-size portions, you are going to love the convenience of this shortcut.

Oh, and don't miss my Anytime Berry Crumble (page 80). It's one of the easiest and best desserts in the world.

# GARLIC BUTTER

GLUTEN-FREE — VEGETARIAN

I panic without garlic butter. Make it once and you'll see what I mean. Try a few dollops melted into my 30-Minute Roasted Tomato Basil Pasta (page 64) or tossed with 10-Minute Garlic-Roasted Asparagus (page 71). It's a super quick way to boost flavor.

PS: To preserve freshness, keep your garlic butter frozen.

## YIELDS ¼ POUND (227 G)

2 sticks or 16 tbsp (227 g) unsalted butter, softened

2–3 fat cloves of garlic, green stem removed

1 tsp coarse salt

¼ cup (15 g) finely chopped parsley

**TIP:** To quickly soften butter, place in a bowl and microwave for about 10–15 seconds or until soft to the touch. Be careful not to melt the butter; it won't set up properly. Another method is to whack the butter (still in its waxy wrapper) with a rolling pin until flat like a pancake—this is fun, actually. Both techniques will take the chill off and blend easily.

To a food processor, add the butter, garlic cloves and salt. Process until smooth.

Using a rubber spatula, scrape the butter into a large bowl and fold in the chopped parsley. I do this by hand, so the butter remains white with flecks of green throughout. If you like your butter the color of Shrek, by all means, throw it into the food processor to blend.

### STORAGE OPTION #1: ROLLED LOGS
Place the butter on a large sheet of parchment paper. Shape into a log, roll it up, and twist the ends to close. Label and date accordingly. Freeze up to 3 months. To use, slice off whatever you need for your recipes.

### STORAGE OPTION #2: TABLESPOON-SIZE PORTIONS
Using a mini ice cream scoop, about 1 inch (2.5 cm) in diameter, portion the butter onto a parchment-lined tray. Freeze until solid, about 15 minutes. Transfer to an airtight container or zip-top bag and label and date accordingly. Freeze up to 3 months.

Yields approximately 16–20 tablespoon-size portions. This is an excellent storage option for when you need an exact measurement (just like stick butter).

**A NOTE ABOUT GARLIC:** My life changed forever after sampling fresh, new season garlic at the Union Square Farmers' Markets in New York City. A vendor rubbed sliced garlic onto warm, toasted sourdough and placed the bread into my hands like a newborn baby (I nearly died from excitement). The flavor was surprisingly soft and not pungent as initially expected. At that moment, I realized not all garlic was created equal. Young garlic is pleasantly mild, and older garlic has a stronger taste.

When choosing the best garlic, look for firm, tight bulbs. Stay away from anything that is soft, sprouting and shedding its white papery skin.

# 30-MINUTE ROASTED TOMATO BASIL PASTA

VEGETARIAN

Whether destined for soup or salad, cherry tomatoes always have a place in my fridge. Oftentimes, they get wrinkly if not used right away. Instead of tossing them, roast the tomatoes in the oven with fresh basil and Garlic Butter (page 63). The heat causes the tomatoes to burst, flooding the pan with the most delicious, flavorful sauce. Toss through with pasta for a quick and easy dinner.

SERVES 4

1 lb (454 g) mezze rigatoni pasta

2 tbsp (30 ml) olive oil, plus more for drizzling

1 lb (454 g) cherry tomatoes

2 cups (48 g) basil leaves, divided

Coarse salt and freshly ground black pepper

4 tbsp (60 g) Garlic Butter (page 63)

Wedge of Parmesan cheese, for grating

Preheat your oven to 425°F (220°C). Find a large roasting pan to fit your tomatoes, a 9 x 13-inch (23 x 33-cm) baking dish should be good.

Bring a pot of water to a boil. Add the pasta and cook according to the package instructions. Drain and set aside. Drizzle with olive oil to prevent sticking.

While the pasta is cooking, add your tomatoes to the roasting pan. Tear 1 cup (24 g) of basil leaves directly over the tomatoes. Add the olive oil and season well with salt and pepper.

Roast for about 25 minutes or until the tomatoes begin to burst and their juices release into the pan. Remove from the oven and add the garlic butter. Toss well to combine. If your garlic butter is frozen, give it a couple of extra minutes to melt.

To serve, add the pasta to a large bowl. Top with your roasted tomatoes, using a rubber spatula to scrape out every last bit of that flavorful sauce. Dust with Parmesan cheese, maybe another drizzle of olive oil, and scatter the remaining 1 cup (24 g) of basil leaves over the top.

# ANGEL HAIR WITH GARLIC & ANCHOVIES

Don't worry. I won't to try to convince you. You either like anchovies or you don't. Melted into a quick pan sauce with fragrant Garlic Butter (page 63) they taste absolutely heavenly. Yes, you read that right—*heavenly.* This dish is an impressive pantry meal that can be whipped up in less than 20 minutes.

PS: I like to cook my pasta in a small amount of water. It boils faster and creates a beautiful starchy liquid used to thicken the pan sauce.

### SERVES 2

2 quarts (2 L) water

½ lb (250 g) angel hair pasta or thin spaghetti

4 tbsp (60 g) Garlic Butter (page 63)

2 tbsp (30 ml) olive oil

4–5 anchovies, packed in oil

½ cup (30 g) roughly chopped parsley

¼ tsp red pepper flakes

Freshly ground black pepper

Bring 2 quarts (2 L) of water to a boil. Add the pasta and cook according to the package instructions. Before draining, reserve ½ cup (118 ml) of the cooking liquid for your pan sauce.

In a large, 12-inch (30-cm) skillet, gently warm the garlic butter and olive oil over low heat. You don't want to burn the garlic, or the sauce will taste bitter. Add the anchovies and stir with a wooden spoon until they melt into the sauce, about 1 minute.

To the pan, add the cooked pasta and toss well with tongs. Get every single strand coated with your delicious sauce. Add about 2 tablespoons (30 ml) of the reserved cooking liquid. The trick here is to keep moving the pasta over low heat so the sauce thickens and is not watery. Add more liquid as needed.

Stir in your fresh parsley, red pepper flakes (add more if you like it spicy) and freshly ground black pepper, to taste. You should be okay with the salt since anchovies themselves lend a salty flavor.

To serve, pile your gorgeous, garlicky angel hair pasta onto plates or shallow bowls.

TIP: The next time you have a giant bunch of parsley, chop the leaves and freeze in a shallow container. Unlike most frozen herbs, the color will stay green up to 3 months. Simply scoop out what you need for your recipes. Freeze the parsley stems, too, for homemade Triple-Duty Chicken Stock (page 27).

# MAKE-AHEAD GARLIC BREAD

VEGETARIAN

What is it about garlic bread that makes people swoon? The bread? The aroma? For me, it's all about getting the proportions right: not too much garlic, good-quality butter and the most delicious bread you can find.

With a stash of homemade Garlic Butter (page 63) on hand, you can make this anytime you want. No need for rubbery, store-bought garlic bread ever again. The preparation is simple and as the name suggests, you can make it ahead. Morph day-old leftovers into epic croutons.

SERVES 6

6 tbsp (90 g) Garlic Butter (page 63)

1 loaf of delicious good-quality crusty bread, such as ciabatta or sourdough

2 tbsp (10 g) ground Parmesan cheese

1 tbsp (4 g) chopped parsley

Preheat your oven to 350°F (175°C). Grab a rimmed baking sheet for your bread.

Add the garlic butter to a small saucepan and melt over low heat, about 1–2 minutes. Be careful not to burn the garlic, or it will taste bitter.

Meanwhile, slice the bread in half lengthwise. Open it up like a book. Carefully brush or spoon the melted butter over both halves, getting into every nook and cranny.

Place the halves on top of each other, wrap in foil and transfer to your rimmed baking sheet.

Bake for about 5–10 minutes to warm through. For extra crunch, unwrap the bread and broil for 1–2 minutes to crisp it up. Keep your eye on it so it doesn't burn!

When cool enough to handle, cut the bread into thick slices. Sprinkle with Parmesan cheese and parsley. Share with friends so you can have garlic breath together. Serve warm.

TIP: To make this ahead of time, simply wrap in foil, then place in a large zip-top bag. Stash in the fridge or freezer until ready to bake.

# 10-MINUTE GARLIC-ROASTED ASPARAGUS

GLUTEN-FREE — VEGETARIAN

Roasted asparagus is an excellent choice for a quick weeknight side dish. Having Garlic Butter (page 63) on hand not only adds delicious flavor, you will be more inclined to use it for all kinds of roasted vegetable recipes. Plus, it's ready in about 10 minutes.

PS: Keep in mind, asparagus will continue to cook once removed from the heat. Always err on the side of underdone to be safe. No one likes mushy veggies!

## SERVES 4, AS A SIDE DISH

1 lb (454 g) medium-size asparagus, about 1 bunch

1 tsp olive oil

Coarse salt and freshly ground black pepper

2 tbsp (30 g) Garlic Butter (page 63)

Preheat your oven to 400°F (200°C). Grab one to two rimmed baking sheets and line with parchment paper.

To prepare the asparagus, snap off the woody ends at the base of each stalk (they are too tough to eat). Place the asparagus on the baking sheet, drizzle with olive oil and season with salt and pepper. Toss with your hands to coat.

Bake the asparagus for about 5 minutes. Add the garlic butter, breaking it up into pieces over the top. Continue to roast for another 2–5 minutes or until the asparagus is tender.

Remove the tray from the oven, and give the asparagus a quick toss to drink in the garlic butter.

Serve warm to accompany your meal.

# ONE-POT GARLIC & HERB POTATOES

GLUTEN-FREE — VEGETARIAN

One year, I was feeling rather ambitious and grew my own potatoes in the backyard. And I learned an interesting fact: *homegrown potatoes cook faster than grocery store potatoes.* According to my CSA farmer, this is because fresh potatoes have a higher water content. Now, of course, you do not need to grow your own potatoes to make this recipe (can you imagine?). I'm telling you this because cooking times will vary.

For this recipe, the entire steaming method is conveniently done in a Dutch oven on the stove. Garlic Butter (page 63) adds instant flavor and in about 30–50 minutes, you'll have beautiful, soft and creamy potatoes. It is a wonderful and delicate way to enjoy your spuds.

## SERVES 4–6, AS A SIDE DISH

4 tbsp (60 g) Garlic Butter (page 63)

1 lb (454 g) fingerling potatoes, whole

2–3 tbsp (30–45 ml) water

Coarse salt and freshly ground black pepper

2 tbsp (8 g) roughly chopped parsley

In a large Dutch oven, gently melt the garlic butter over low heat. Add the potatoes and 2 tablespoons (30 ml) of water. Season with salt and pepper and mix well to combine.

Place the lid on top and "steam" for about 30 to 50 minutes. Cooking time will vary depending on size and freshness of your potatoes. Have a peek inside every now and then to make sure the potatoes are not browning too fast. Quick Tip: Add an additional splash of water to slow down cooking.

To check for doneness, insert a small paring knife into the center of a potato; if it comes out easily, they're ready. If there is resistance, continue to cook until soft.

When the potatoes are done to your liking, add the chopped parsley. Give them a quick toss and serve warm.

# CINNAMON SUGAR BUTTER

GLUTEN-FREE — VEGETARIAN

This brings me right back to my childhood. Warm cinnamon sugar on toast…. The flavor is pleasantly sweet with just the right amount of cinnamon. I like to freeze compound butters to preserve freshness; however, keep a small stash in the fridge to quickly spread on muffins and toast and to make Convenient Crumbles (page 79).

## YIELDS ½ POUND (227 G)

2 sticks or 16 tbsp (227 g) unsalted butter, softened

¼ cup (50 g) sugar

2 tbsp (16 g) cinnamon

½ tsp fine sea salt

To a food processor, add the butter, sugar, cinnamon and salt. Process until well blended. Use a rubber spatula to scrape down the sides of the bowl.

### STORAGE OPTION #1: ROLLED LOGS

Place the butter on a large sheet of parchment paper. Shape into a log, roll it up, and twist the ends to close. Label and date accordingly. Freeze up to 3 months. To use, slice off whatever you need for your recipes.

### STORAGE OPTION #2: TABLESPOON-SIZE PORTIONS

Using a mini ice cream scoop, about 1 inch (2.5 cm) in diameter, portion the butter onto a parchment-lined tray. Freeze until solid, about 10–15 minutes. Transfer to an airtight container or zip-top bag and label and date accordingly. Freeze up to 3 months.

Yields approximately 16–20 tablespoon-size portions. This is an excellent storage option for when you need an exact measurement (just like stick butter).

TIP: To quickly soften butter, place the butter in a bowl and microwave for about 10–15 seconds or until soft to the touch. Be careful not to melt the butter; it won't set up properly. Another method is to whack the butter (still in its waxy wrapper) with a rolling pin until flat like a pancake. Both techniques will take the chill off and blend easily.

# 5-MINUTE SKILLET GRANOLA

VEGETARIAN

Because I love a good culinary challenge, I've come up with an easier way to make granola.

Using *quick oats* is my secret ingredient. They're partially cooked, which means they absorb liquid quickly. Just watch as the flecks of dusty beige oats turn golden brown while drinking in the sweet flavor of Cinnamon Sugar Butter (page 75). The smell is fantastic.

Head's up—your granola won't seem very crisp at first. Once it cools it will become wonderfully crunchy.

## MAKES 1 CUP (100 G)

3 tbsp (45 g) Cinnamon Sugar Butter (page 75)

1 tbsp (21 g) honey

1 cup (80 g) quick oats (not instant or old fashioned rolled oats)

¼ cup (30 g) chopped walnuts

In a nonstick skillet, melt the cinnamon sugar butter over medium heat. Grab a large plate or tray and line with parchment paper.

Add the honey to the pan and swirl to coat. Pour in your oats, stirring constantly until the color changes from beige to golden brown. This will happen quickly, anywhere from 3-4 minutes. Add the walnuts at the very end to lightly toast.

Spread out the granola, in one single layer, on your lined plate. It will crisp up as it cools.

To preserve freshness, refrigerate your granola in an airtight container up to 1 week. Freeze up to 3 months.

TIP: This granola is wonderful for holiday or hostess gifts packaged in mason jars. Try playing around with different ingredients such as nutmeg, ground ginger and luscious flavored honeys to enhance flavor.

# CONVENIENT CRUMBLES

VEGETARIAN

Who doesn't love a good fruit crumble dessert? The topping is the best part! Keep a stash of these sweet, cinnamon sugar crumbles in the freezer and whip up a delicious Anytime Berry Crumble (page 80) in a matter of minutes. This is one of my favorite shortcuts.

PS: This recipe yields more than enough crumbles for two 9 x 13-inch (23 x 33-cm) baking dishes.

## MAKES APPROXIMATELY 5½ CUPS (715 G)

1 cup or 16 tbsp (227 g) Cinnamon Sugar Butter (page 75), softened

2 cups (250 g) flour

1 cup (220 g) light brown sugar, packed

1 cup (80 g) old fashioned rolled oats

Add all of the ingredients to a large bowl. Mix together by hand until crumbles start to form (keep mixing until the flour is no longer visible). Squeeze together for big crumbles or keep them small and sandy.

Transfer to airtight containers or zip-top bags, label and date. Freeze up to 3 months. No need to defrost before using.

# ANYTIME BERRY CRUMBLE

VEGETARIAN

This is one of the easiest desserts in the world. There's no cake to frost, filling to set or finicky dough to roll. And it takes only two minutes to prep. Simply add frozen berries to a baking dish, sprinkle with sugar and top with Convenient Crumbles (page 79). Bake until hot and bubbly. Just don't skip out on the ice cream or crème fraîche.

See the variation at the end of the recipe for a delicious apple crumble. Because really, when it comes to dessert, less is *never* more.

## SERVES 6, OR 4 GREEDY PEOPLE

Small pat of unsalted butter, for coating the pan

1 (16-oz [454-g]) bag of frozen mixed berries

2 tbsp (25 g) sugar

1 tbsp (8 g) cornstarch

2½ cups (325 g) Convenient Crumbles (page 79)

Vanilla ice cream or crème fraîche, to serve

Preheat your oven to 350°F (175°C). Lightly coat a 9 x 13-inch (23 x 33-cm) baking pan with butter.

To a large bowl, add the frozen berries. Sprinkle with sugar and cornstarch, then mix together to combine—I do this with my hands. Tip the fruit into your coated baking pan, and casually sprinkle your crumbles over the top.

Bake for about 30–40 minutes. Your dessert is ready when the top is perfectly golden and the fruit is hot and bubbly.

Serve warm, with a scoop of vanilla ice cream or crème fraîche for the ultimate indulgence.

TIP: Try this the next day (cold) with a dollop of thick Greek yogurt for breakfast. Mmm.

VARIATION: Cut up 4-5 Granny Smith apples (peeled) into 2-inch (5-cm) pieces. Toss with ¼ cup (50 g) sugar and 1 teaspoon cinnamon. Top with 2½ cups (325 g) Convenient Crumbles (page 79) and bake as directed above.

*chapter four*

# HOMEMADE SPICE BLENDS

Thirty-two. That was the number of spice jars crammed into my kitchen cabinet. It's a deep corner cabinet, which is like a black hole (a recent search for dried oregano unearthed a handful of Legos, okay?). After inadvertently dumping Madras curry powder onto my son's French toast one morning, I'd had enough.

To get organized, I condensed most of my spices into two master blends. My Everyday Spice Blend (page 85) is versatile, and my go-to seasoning of choice beyond salt and pepper. My Mexican Spice Blend (page 97) is perfect for more boldly flavored recipes and, of course, typical Mexican or Tex-Mex fare.

By customizing your own blends, you are free from preservatives and funky ingredients hidden in the mix. Care for some MSG? Homemade blends also give you control over different seasoning combinations, including the amount of salt.

And another great benefit? You are simplifying your cooking routine! No more time wasted searching for spices; no more dumping curry powder onto French toast because you thought it was cinnamon; no more reliance on expensive, store-bought blends.

This shortcut is easy. It's a great way to use up what you have on hand, plus a possible addition or two. Try these all-purpose blends on Skillet Stuffed Chicken with Spinach & Ricotta (page 86), Heaven on the Cob (page 105) and my Fast Shrimp Tacos (page 102).

# EVERYDAY SPICE BLEND

GLUTEN-FREE — VEGETARIAN — VEGAN

This is a versatile blend with light notes of garlic and sweet smoky paprika. Ground coriander is my secret ingredient for a hint of citrus flavor. It's a pleasant marriage; one does not dominate the other. Try this on just about everything.

## MAKES APPROXIMATELY ¼ CUP (25 G)

2 tbsp (17 g) coarse salt

½ tsp garlic powder

¼ tsp sweet smoked paprika

¼ tsp ground coriander

Add all of the ingredients to a small mixing bowl. Whisk thoroughly to combine. Store in an airtight container or mason jar, label and date. It will last 6 months to 1 year stored in a cool, dry place.

TIP: If you have time, lightly toast any "vintage" spices in a dry pan to revitalize their flavors. It will only take a minute or two.

# SKILLET STUFFED CHICKEN WITH SPINACH & RICOTTA

**GLUTEN-FREE**

Doesn't everything sound better with ricotta? This is a great fallback meal. It's easy to prep with minimal ingredients. A delicious dinner is ready in 30–40 minutes.

To save time, use frozen chopped spinach. It has more bulk than fresh spinach, making it perfect for fillings. Plus, you don't have to sauté it first. A sprinkle of Everyday Spice Blend (page 85) is added for flavor, and the entire skillet is baked in the oven. Did I mention, there's only one pan to clean?

## SERVES 4

1 (10-oz [284-g]) box frozen chopped spinach, thawed

½ cup (123 g) ricotta

Coarse salt and freshly ground black pepper

4 boneless, skinless, chicken breasts

Everyday Spice Blend (page 85)

1 tbsp (15 ml) olive oil, plus more as needed

1 heaped cup (150 g) colorful cherry tomatoes, halved

1 tbsp (15 g) unsalted butter

Preheat your oven to 425°F (220°C).

Place the thawed spinach on a clean kitchen towel. Twist up to close, and squeeze out as much liquid as possible. The spinach should be nice and dry. In a bowl, combine the spinach with ricotta and season with salt and pepper. Mix well.

Slice your chicken lengthwise, about three-quarters of the way in to create a pocket.

Stuff each chicken breast with a portion of the spinach and ricotta filling, pushing it in as far back as it will go. This way, it won't spill out into the pan. Alternatively, tie up the chicken breasts with kitchen twine. Sprinkle with Everyday Spice Blend.

In a large, 12-inch (30-cm) oven-proof skillet, warm the olive oil over medium heat. Sear the chicken for 3–4 minutes on each side, transferring to a plate as you go.

Place the chicken back in your skillet. Scatter the halved cherry tomatoes all around the pan. Add the butter, breaking it up into small pieces.

Transfer the skillet to the oven, and bake until the chicken is cooked through and the tomatoes begin to lose their shape, about 7–10 minutes. Quick Tip: Cooking times will vary based on the size of your chicken. Have a look at the 7-minute mark to double check.

To serve, portion your stuffed chicken onto plates, spooning the delicious blistered tomato sauce over the top.

# SHEET PAN FISH & CHIPS

GLUTEN-FREE

Anything cooked on a sheet pan rules in my book. It's that one-pan, minimal-cleanup that draws me in for the win. Here, dinner is made easier with Everyday Spice Blend (page 85) for instant flavor. The fish and chips are baked side by side until perfectly golden, and then topped with lemon-dressed arugula.

PS: You might find yourself eating the dill sauce while waiting for the fish to cook. It's that good.

## SERVES 4

1½ lbs (680 g) wild-caught cod, center cut about 1½-inch (3.8-cm) thick

2 tsp (10 ml) olive oil

Everyday Spice Blend (page 85)

### HAND-CUT CHIPS

3 medium russet potatoes, skin on, cut into 20–24 wedges total

2 tbsp (30 ml) olive oil

Coarse salt and freshly ground black pepper

### DILL SAUCE

¼ cup (60 ml) mayonnaise

¼ cup (50 g) Greek yogurt

¼ cup diced pickles

1 tbsp (3 g) chopped dill

2 lemons, cut into wedges

2 handfuls of baby arugula leaves, for serving

Preheat your oven to 425°F (220°C). Line a rimmed baking sheet with parchment paper.

Remove the fish from the fridge, and blot with a paper towel to remove any excess moisture. Drizzle lightly with olive oil and season with Everyday Spice Blend. Set aside on the counter to take the chill off while you cut the potatoes.

In a large bowl, toss the potato wedges with olive oil. Season lightly with salt and pepper. Spread out evenly, in one single layer, onto your baking sheet.

Roast the potatoes for about 30–35 minutes, turning once at the 15-minute mark. Also at the 15-minute mark, add the fish to the pan. Scoot the potatoes over to make room for the cod. Roast for an additional 15–20 minutes. The fish is ready when it's fully cooked though, firm and beginning to flake apart—poke with a fork to check.

Meanwhile, combine the dill sauce ingredients in a small bowl. Cover and chill until ready to use. Cut your lemons into wedges.

When ready to eat, gather everyone around and place your baked fish and chips in the center of the table. Top with arugula leaves and a squeeze of lemon. Serve with your chilled dill sauce on the side.

TIP: As an alternative to cod, try this with salmon or halibut instead.

# WARM SWEET POTATO SALAD WITH BACON & GOAT CHEESE

This salad is great for entertaining. In fact, I've served it at Thanksgiving a couple of times. To cut down on prep, skip peeling the sweet potatoes and tear up the country bread with your hands. It's much faster this way. Then roast everything together and toss with baby greens right before serving. If you have any leftover quinoa in the fridge, throw that in too—it will add a delicious and subtle nutty flavor.

## SERVES 4-6, AS A SIDE DISH

2 slices of country bread, such as sourdough

3 cups (400 g) sweet potatoes, skin on, cut into 1-inch (2.5-cm) cubes

¼ cup (60 ml) olive oil

Everyday Spice Blend (page 85)

4 slices of bacon, cut into 1-inch (2.5-cm) pieces

### MAPLE-DIJON JAM JAR DRESSING

1 tsp Dijon mustard

1 tbsp (15 ml) maple syrup

¼ cup (60 ml) red wine vinegar

½ cup (118 ml) olive oil

Coarse salt and freshly ground pepper

5 oz (142 g) mixed baby greens

½ cup (60 g) mixed dried fruit such as figs, cherries or cranberries

1 cup (185 g) cooked quinoa, room temperature (optional)*

½ cup (136 g) crumbled goat cheese

*Approximately ¼ cup (40 g) dry quinoa yields 1 cup (185 g) cooked*

Preheat your oven to 375°F (190°C). Line a rimmed baking sheet with parchment paper.

Working directly over a large bowl, tear up the country bread using your hands. Add the sweet potatoes. Drizzle with olive oil and season with Everyday Spice Blend. Toss well.

Tip the mixture onto your lined baking sheet, spreading it out into one single layer. Scatter the sliced bacon over the top.

Roast for about 20 minutes, turning once, until everything is golden brown.

Meanwhile, make the dressing. Add the first four ingredients to an empty jam jar. Season with salt and pepper. Screw the lid on tight and shake (like you mean it) to blend.

When the sweet potatoes are soft and the bacon is golden, remove from the oven. Cool for about 5 minutes before adding the greens. Try a bite—it's really good.

When ready to serve, add your baby greens directly to the baking sheet. Sprinkle with dried fruit, quinoa (if using) and drizzle lightly with dressing. Crumble the goat cheese over the top and toss gently to combine.

Serve warm or at room temperature.

# 15-MINUTE GRILLED SKIRT STEAK & SALAD

GLUTEN-FREE

At least once a week, my cousin Elise and I get together for dinner. There are five kids between us (mostly boys), ranging anywhere from 4–10 years old. It's *loud.* We battle the chaos by keeping dinner simple.

Quickly flavored with Everyday Spice Blend (page 85), a thin piece of skirt steak takes only about 6 minutes to cook for medium rare. It's quick and reliably juicy every time. Combined with a fresh green salad studded with dried cranberries and feta, this is an easy and satisfying 15-minute meal.

SERVES 4

2 lbs (907 g) skirt steak

1 tsp vegetable oil

Everyday Spice Blend (page 85)

BALSAMIC JAM JAR VINAIGRETTE

1 tbsp (15 ml) balsamic vinegar

¼ cup (60 ml) red wine vinegar

½ cup (118 ml) olive oil

Coarse salt and freshly ground black pepper

SALAD

5 oz (142 g) mixed baby greens

½ cup (60 g) dried cranberries

½ cup (55 g) chopped walnuts, almonds or pecans

½ cup (75 g) crumbled feta

Preheat your grill to high heat. Lightly coat the skirt steak with vegetable oil and season with Everyday Spice Blend.

To make the vinaigrette, add the first three ingredients to an empty jam jar. Season with salt and pepper. Screw the lid on tight and shake well to blend.

For the salad, add your baby greens to a large bowl. Sprinkle with dried cranberries, chopped nuts and crumbled feta. Toss lightly with some of the dressing and set aside.

Place the skirt steak on the grill. Cook for about 3 minutes per side for medium rare. If you'd like your steak medium temperature, cook for an additional minute or two longer. When the steak is grilled to your liking, transfer to a large cutting board. Allow the meat to rest for at least 5 minutes for the juices to redistribute.

To serve, slice the meat against the grain and enjoy with your leafy green salad on the side.

# SWEET & SAVORY SPICED NUTS

GLUTEN-FREE — VEGETARIAN

If you need a quick snack or a party nibble for guests, these spiced nuts will be a guaranteed hit. It's a great way to transform your Everyday Spice Blend (page 85) into something unique, and in this case, a light dusting of curry powder and cinnamon does the trick.

Instead of purchasing multiple bags of nuts, grab a bag of *mixed* nuts for variety. If you're really clever, rummage through your cabinets to see what you already have on hand. You will need about 4 cups (454 g) of mixed nuts total.

PS: Make sure to use unsalted nuts in this recipe (see tip below).

## MAKES 4 CUPS (454 G)

2 tbsp (30 ml) water

1 tbsp (15 g) unsalted butter

¼ cup (55 g) brown sugar

1 heaped tsp Everyday Spice Blend (page 85)

¼ tsp cinnamon

¼ tsp curry powder

1 lb (454 g) bag of mixed nuts, roasted and unsalted

Line a rimmed baking sheet with parchment paper—you will need this for your nuts to cool.

In a large nonstick skillet, melt the water, butter and sugar over low heat. Bring the mixture to a gentle boil, and simmer to throughly dissolve the sugar, about 2–3 minutes. Add the Everyday Spice Blend, cinnamon and curry powder. Mix well.

Add the nuts and stir constantly. They should be well coated in the spiced glaze mixture.

Pour the mixture onto your lined baking sheet. Cool for 5–10 minutes for the glaze to harden and set.

Store your sweet and savory nuts in an airtight container in the fridge, up to 3 weeks.

TIP: Because there is salt in the Everyday Spice Blend, remember to use unsalted mixed nuts and unsalted butter, or else you will be guzzling a sports drink to rehydrate.

# MEXICAN SPICE BLEND

GLUTEN-FREE — VEGETARIAN — VEGAN

This blend is sightly spicy, not too salty and perfectly zesty for Mexican and Tex-Mex recipes.

## MAKES APPROXIMATELY ½ CUP (50 G)

2 tsp (6 g) coarse salt

2 tsp (4 g) cumin

Pinch of cayenne pepper

2 tbsp (15 g) chili powder

1 tbsp (7 g) sweet smoked paprika

1 tbsp (8 g) garlic powder

1 tbsp (7 g) onion powder

1 tbsp (3 g) dried oregano

Add all of the ingredients to a small mixing bowl. Whisk thoroughly to combine. Store in an airtight container or mason jar, label and date. It will last 6 months to 1 year stored in a cool, dry place.

TIP: If you have time, lightly toast any "vintage" spices in a dry pan to revitalize their flavors. It will only take a minute or two.

# SIMPLE SPICE-ROASTED CARROT & AVOCADO SALAD

GLUTEN-FREE — VEGETARIAN — VEGAN

Have you tried roasted carrots and avocados together? What a smashing pair. The carrots are dusted in Mexican Spice Blend (page 97) for fast flavor and tossed with waxy pine nuts and plump, sweet golden raisins. The avocado, always welcome in my kitchen, offers an addicting creaminess. Serve as a unique side dish with grilled meat and fish. Simple, easy and delicious!

## SERVES 2–4, AS A SIDE DISH

4 medium carrots, peeled and cut into 1-inch (2.5-cm) pieces

1 tbsp (15 ml) olive oil, plus more for drizzling

1 heaped tsp Mexican Spice Blend (page 97)

2 tbsp (15 g) pine nuts

¼ cup (40 g) golden raisins

1 ripe Hass avocado

Juice of ½ lemon

Pinch of salt

Large handful of micro greens, sprouts or baby mesclun

Preheat your oven to 425°F (220°C). Line a rimmed baking sheet with parchment paper.

Place the carrots in a large bowl. Add the olive oil and sprinkle with Mexican Spice Blend. Toss well to coat. Spread the carrots out on your sheet pan.

Roast for about 20 minutes, or until the carrots are caramelized and tender. Remove from the oven, and add the pine nuts and raisins. Give it a good stir. Allow the carrots to cool slightly.

While the carrots are cooling, dice up the avocado. Drizzle with lemon juice to prevent browning and season with a pinch of salt. Add the avocados and greens to the carrots, and toss gently to combine. Finish with extra lemon juice and a drizzle of olive oil to taste.

Serve at room temperature rustic style, directly on the baking sheet.

# DAD'S QUICK GREEK FAJITA FLATBREADS

Take one bite and you'll find yourself somewhere in between a sizzling fajita and a Greek souvlaki. My dad came up with this creative combo using Mexican Spice Blend (page 97) as a clever shortcut; there's no time wasted searching for a gazillion herbs and spices (where's the cumin?!). The homemade tzatziki is a cool and refreshing accompaniment.

SERVES 4

4 flatbreads

TZATZIKI SAUCE

1 cup (200 g) Greek yogurt

½ cup (67 g) grated cucumber

1 garlic clove, grated

2 tsp (10 ml) red wine vinegar

1 tbsp (3 g) chopped fresh dill

Coarse salt, to taste

1 lb (454 g) boneless, skinless chicken breasts, thinly sliced

1 tbsp (8 g) Mexican Spice Blend (page 97)

2 tbsp (30 ml) olive oil, divided

2 sweet bell peppers, mixed colors, thinly sliced

½ juicy lime

TOPPINGS

1 cup (150 g) cherry tomatoes, halved

½ cup (30 g) parsley leaves

1-2 juicy limes, cut into wedges

Preheat your oven to 200°F (90°C). Wrap the flatbreads in a clean, damp kitchen towel and place onto a rimmed baking sheet. Warm gently in the oven until you are ready to eat.

Combine the tzatziki sauce ingredients into a small bowl. Add more salt or vinegar if necessary; it should taste bright and punchy. Cover and chill until ready to use.

In a large bowl, add the chicken and sprinkle with the Mexican Spice Blend. Toss well and keep handy on the counter.

In a large, 10-inch (25-cm) cast-iron skillet, warm 1 tablespoon (15 ml) of olive oil over medium heat. Sauté the peppers until golden, about 3–4 minutes. Transfer to a plate.

To the skillet, add the remaining 1 tablespoon (15 ml) of olive oil. Sauté the chicken until cooked through, about 3–5 minutes. Work in batches if necessary. Add the peppers back to the pan with the chicken. Crank up the heat and give it a good stir. Squeeze in the juice of ½ lime. You will get a nice fajita-style sizzle.

To serve, remove your flatbreads from the oven. Portion the chicken and pepper mixture onto each flatbread. Top with cherry tomatoes, parsley leaves and a couple of lime wedges. Have your chilled tzatziki sauce ready to go on the side.

# FAST SHRIMP TACOS

GLUTEN-FREE OPTION

If you could wrap up summer in a warm tortilla blanket, you'd get these quick shrimp tacos. They take about 5–10 minutes to prep, and only a few minutes to cook. It's a fun play on textures, highlighting cool and refreshing cucumbers, juicy tomatoes and creamy goat cheese. The only thing missing is the Coronas....

## SERVES 4

1½ lbs (680 g) peeled and deveined shrimp, tail off

2 tbsp (30 ml) olive oil, divided

1 tbsp (8 g) Mexican Spice Blend (page 97)

Zest of 1 lime

### CUCUMBER TOMATO SALSA

1 cup (133 g) diced cucumbers

1 small tomato, diced

2 tbsp (2 g) chopped cilantro

Coarse salt and freshly ground black pepper

8 small flour tortillas (or corn tortillas for gluten-free)

½ cup (136 g) crumbled goat cheese

1–2 juicy limes, cut into wedges

Remove the shrimp from its packaging and pat dry with paper towels. The olive oil and spices will stick better this way, and the shrimp will get a good sear.

Add the shrimp to a bowl. Drizzle with 1 tablespoon (15 ml) of olive oil and sprinkle with the Mexican Spice Blend. Grate the lime zest directly over the top. Toss well to coat.

While the shrimp is marinating, chop your veggies for the salsa. Add the cucumber, tomatoes and cilantro to a small bowl and season lightly with salt and pepper. Quick Tip: The salt will draw out the natural water in the cucumbers and tomatoes; drain it off before serving.

In a large, 10-inch (25-cm) cast-iron skillet, warm the remaining 1 tablespoon (15 ml) of olive oil over medium heat. Sauté the shrimp until bright pink and cooked through, about 2–4 minutes.

When you're ready to eat, fill each tortilla with your flavorful Mexican shrimp. Top with the cucumber tomato salsa, goat cheese and lime wedges on the side.

TIP: Limes are incredibly stingy when it comes to their juice. Always buy a few extra. Before slicing, give them a good roll on the counter or microwave for 5 seconds to loosen up the fruit. If you are desperate, a citrus juicer or reamer will work too.

# HEAVEN ON THE COB

GLUTEN-FREE — VEGETARIAN

Char-grilled to smoky perfection, slathered in lime-scented yogurt and topped with Parmesan cheese? Yes, please! The secret is mixing a dash of Mexican Spice Blend (page 97) directly into the yogurt for fast flavor—it's what makes this dish. If you have yet to try a single thing from this cookbook, start here. Any leftovers would make a wonderful addition to my Southwestern Quinoa Salad (page 162).

SERVES 4–6

4-6 ears of fresh sweet corn

1 tsp vegetable oil

## LIME YOGURT SAUCE

¼ cup (60 ml) mayonnaise

¼ cup (50 g) Greek yogurt

1 tsp Mexican Spice Blend (page 97)

Zest and juice of ½ lime

## TOPPINGS

¼ cup (25 g) ground Parmesan cheese

1 juicy lime, cut into wedges

Preheat your grill to high heat. Shuck the corn, leaving the bottom portion intact as your "handle." If you'd like, save some of the leaves for serving (see picture). Drizzle lightly with vegetable oil to coat.

Place the corn on the grill and close the lid. Lightly char on all sides turning every 2–3 minutes. Your corn should be ready in about 8–12 minutes total. To check for doneness, sample a corn kernel. It should taste sweet and tender.

Meanwhile, make the lime yogurt sauce. Combine all of the ingredients in a bowl and whisk well to combine. Give it a taste, adding more lime juice if needed to make the flavors pop.

Transfer your smoky grilled corn to a platter. Cool for about 1–2 minutes before adding the sauce. The aroma will be pleasantly warm and nutty, almost like popcorn.

When ready to eat, spread some of the lime yogurt sauce onto each ear of corn. Sprinkle with Parmesan cheese. Serve on a bed of corn leaves with juicy lime wedges on the side.

*chapter five*

# EASY BEANS

Frustrating isn't it?

You barely have time to brush your teeth and now you should cook dried beans from scratch? Why on earth would you want to do that?

Cooking beans from scratch isn't something new; we've been doing it for centuries. Beans and legumes are powerhouse staples consumed in diets across the globe. In comparison to their canned counterparts, dried beans are more flavorful and, economically speaking, they're actually cheaper! Dried beans are essential to any homemade kitchen.

*But using canned is just too easy.*

And I agree. However, a recent trip to the Caribbean islands was an unexpected game changer. No matter what we ordered when dining out, rice and beans was served as an accompaniment. Sometimes it was black beans, sometimes kidney beans—all delicious and beautifully seasoned. They tasted *fresh*. By day five of our trip, rice and beans with sliced avocado on top was my preferred main meal.

*But is it really worth it?*

In this chapter, I've come up with strategies for cooking dried beans on the stove top or in a slow cooker with accessible storage options. Forgot to soak overnight? I've got you covered there too. I specifically focus on three types of beans to get you started. Then you'll learn how to make My Favorite Black Bean Soup (page 124), Stove-Top Maple Baked Beans (page 119) and an Easy Chickpea Caprese Salad (page 112).

If you're curious to taste what's on the other side of a tin can, you've got to try cooking dried beans from scratch. It's like biting into a juicy, summer tomato after a long and miserable winter.

# YOUR DRIED-BEAN GUIDE

In this chapter, you'll learn how to work with three different varieties of dried beans: chickpeas, cannellini and black beans. While the initial preparation for these beans is similar, cooking time will vary according to variety.

## SORTING

Before you begin...

Sometimes, you'll find small rocks and unwanted debris hiding in your dried beans. Quickly dump them out onto a tray, sort through and discard anything that's not supposed to be there.

## TO SOAK OR NOT TO SOAK?

Soaking beans is not hard; it's *remembering* to soak that's the issue.

Try doing this at night when you are making your coffee for the following morning, or while cleaning up the dinner dishes. I keep my beans next to the coffee pot as a friendly reminder. I never forget about my coffee....

### How to Soak Beans

Add dried beans to a large glass or ceramic bowl and cover with warm water, about 3 inches (7.5 cm) above the beans. Soak at room temperature for about 6–8 hours or overnight.

### Why Bother?

Soaking is necessary to par-soften your beans, which will reduce overall cooking time. Also, to receive the nutritional benefits, it's necessary to release the sugars and anti-nutrients. I've also heard that soaking reduces flatulence, although my research proves otherwise (I live with boys).

### What If I Forget to Soak?

Do a quick soak. Simply place the beans in a large pot, cover with water and bring to a boil. Remove from the heat and "steam" (lid on) for about 1 hour to soften. Skim away any foam.

As an alternative to soaking, cook dried beans in a slow cooker. The low and slow heat will get the job done without having to soak.

# COOKING METHODS

## Stove Top

Drain your soaked beans in a colander and rinse well. Add to a large soup pot and cover with about 2–3 inches (5–7.5 cm) of water. Bring the pot to a gentle boil and simmer, stirring occasionally, for about 1–2 hours depending on the variety. Add additional water as needed. Skim away any foam that floats to the top.

## No-Soak Beans for the Slow Cooker

Add your dry, unsoaked beans to a 6-quart (6-L) slow cooker and cover with about 2–3 inches (5–7.5 cm) of water. Cook on high for about 2–4 hours, checking for doneness at the 2–3-hour mark. Alternatively, cook on low for about 5–6 hours, checking for doneness at the 5-hour mark. Cooking time will vary based on the variety.

Regardless of cooking method, your beans are ready when they are soft and tender, not mushy. The beans will not look like soup but rather "cooked" with a bit of liquid sitting at the bottom.

Cool the beans directly in the pot. Do not drain.

NOTE: Unlike pasta, never add salt to the beans while they cook. It toughens the outer skin preventing the beans from becoming soft. Wait until the end to season. However, you are more than welcome to throw in some bay leaves, whole peeled garlic cloves, carrots or even a couple of halved onions to flavor.

## Cooking Times for Beans

| 1 LB (454 G) DRIED BEANS | STOVE TOP (SOAKED) | SLOW-COOKER (UNSOAKED) | YIELD |
|---|---|---|---|
| Chickpeas | 1–1½ hours | 2–4 hours on high/5–6 hours on low | 6 cups (985 g) |
| Cannellini Beans | 1–1½ hours | 2–4 hours on high/5–6 hours on low | 6 cups (1 kg) |
| Black Beans | 2 hours | 2–4 hours on high/5–6 hours on low | 6 cups (1 kg) |

# STORAGE

Storing beans should be convenient and provide easy access for use. Whichever option you choose, make sure the beans are completely cool before storing to prevent unfriendly bacteria.

## Refrigerate

Place beans in their cooking liquid (enough to submerge) in airtight containers and label and date accordingly. Refrigerate up to 3 days. Any longer, and they'll start to get stinky. I'll usually keep 2 cups (344 g) of beans in the fridge, similar to a 15-ounce (425-g) can, and freeze the rest.

## Freeze

Place the beans in their cooking liquid (enough to submerge) in shallow containers or zip-top bags. If using bags, store them flat in the freezer. They will defrost faster and take up less space. Label and date accordingly. Again, I like to divide my beans into 2-cup (344-g) portions, similar to a 15-ounce (425-g) can, for convenient usage. Defrost in the microwave or submerge into a bowl of cold water until fully thawed.

## Canning

You will need a pressure cooker/canner for this method. Because all appliances vary, refer to your manufacturer's instructions for specific details on the correct procedure for canning cooked beans.

NOTE: Though I believe beans cooked from scratch taste much better than canned, it's okay if you need to use canned beans. My hope is to give you options. The recipes will come together just as easily either way. For each recipe that calls for cooked beans, I've included the canned equivalent you would need.

# EASY CHICKPEA CAPRESE SALAD

GLUTEN-FREE — VEGETARIAN

Say hello to the ultimate summer picnic salad! It's easy to make, travels well and is one of those recipes that improves as it sits (don't you wish we could all age that way?). Keep your cooked chickpeas handy in the fridge or freezer, and this Italian-inspired combo will come together in just about 30 minutes.

I'm always on the lookout for new ways to use mint as the giant stalks rage through my garden strangling everything in their path. It works beautifully here, complementing the juicy, basil-scented tomatoes.

## SERVES 6

**BALSAMIC JAM JAR DRESSING**

1 tbsp (15 ml) balsamic vinegar

¼ cup (60 ml) red wine vinegar

½ cup (118 ml) olive oil

Coarse salt and freshly ground black pepper

3 cups (492 g) cooked chickpeas, rinsed & drained*

½ lb (227 g) assorted colorful cherry tomatoes, halved

1 cup (100 g) thinly sliced celery

½ cup (75 g) crumbled feta

2 cups (454 g) mini fresh mozzarella balls

¼ cup (6 g) packed fresh basil leaves

¼ cup (6 g) packed fresh mint leaves

*For more information on cooking dried chickpeas, see pages 109–111, or substitute with one and a half 15-ounce (425-g) cans of chickpeas.*

To make the dressing, add the first three ingredients to an empty jam jar. Season with salt and pepper. Screw the lid on tight and shake vigorously to blend.

For the salad, add the chickpeas, cherry tomatoes, celery, feta and mozzarella to a large serving bowl. Toss well to combine.

Stack the basil leaves on top of each other and roll them up. Cut across into thin ribbons. Do the same for the mint. Sprinkle the fresh herbs onto the salad.

Right before serving, lightly drizzle the salad with the dressing. Taste and season with salt and pepper if necessary. Keep extra dressing handy on the side to serve. Enjoy at room temperature.

TIP: To get ahead, this salad can be made up to 1 day in advance, minus the tomatoes and herbs. Slice the tomatoes, basil and mint on the day that you are going to serve to preserve freshness. The jam jar dressing can also be made in advance, up to 2 weeks in the fridge.

# COCONUT CURRIED CHICKPEAS WITH WILTED GREENS

GLUTEN-FREE — VEGETARIAN — VEGAN

This is a brilliant weeknight dinner. It's quick, flavorful and healthy. Having diced onions on hand from Pre-Chopped Vegetables (page 11), makes it come together even faster (I scoop some onions out of the freezer). The fragrant aroma of sweet coconut and warm curry spices will fill your kitchen in the most tantalizing way. It smells like vacation. Handfuls of tender baby spinach wilt into the broth at the end.

## SERVES 4

2 tbsp (30 ml) olive oil

1 cup (160 g) diced onion

1 clove of garlic, grated

2 tsp (3.5 g) curry powder

1 (14-oz [414-ml]) can of coconut milk

2 cups (328 g) cooked chickpeas, rinsed and drained*

Coarse salt and freshly ground black pepper

2–3 large handfuls of baby spinach

Juice of ½ lemon

Whole-grains, to serve (optional)

*For more information on cooking dried chickpeas, see pages 109–111, or substitute with one 15-ounce (425-g) can of chickpeas.

Warm the olive oil in a large, 10-inch (25-cm) cast-iron or regular skillet. Sauté the onion until soft, about 3–5 minutes. Add the garlic and stir until fragrant, 30 seconds. Add the curry powder and continue to cook for 30 seconds to toast the spices. If at any point the curry gets a little dry, add a splash of water to loosen it up.

To the pan, add the coconut milk and chickpeas. Simmer gently for about 10 minutes, uncovered, stirring occasionally. Season with salt and pepper, to taste.

Add the spinach one handful at a time; the heat from the coconut milk will gently wilt the leaves. Add lemon juice to brighten the flavor.

Portion your curry into shallow bowls and serve with your choice of whole-grains, if desired.

# SPEEDY SMASHED MEDITERRANEAN CHICKPEAS

GLUTEN-FREE OPTION — VEGETARIAN — VEGAN

Soft, home-cooked chickpeas are combined with juicy tomatoes, shallots and capers, for a speedy, no-cook side dish. Part of the fun is smashing the chickpeas for a playful combination of textures. It's excellent with chicken and fish, or simply served with good crusty bread as a light lunch or appetizer.

## SERVES 4

**RED WINE–DIJON JAM JAR DRESSING**

1 tsp Dijon or country mustard

3 tbsp (45 ml) red wine vinegar

½ cup (120 ml) olive oil

Coarse salt and freshly ground black pepper

2 cups (328 g) cooked chickpeas, rinsed and drained*

1 cup (150 g) cherry tomatoes, halved

1 medium shallot, thinly sliced

1 tbsp (9 g) brined capers, rinsed

½ cup (30 g) roughly chopped parsley

1 loaf of good crusty bread, such as whole-grain or sourdough (optional)

*For more information on cooking dried chickpeas, see pages 109–111, or substitute with one 15-ounce (425-g) can of chickpeas.*

To make the dressing, add the first three ingredients to an empty jam jar. Season with salt and pepper. Screw the lid on tight and shake well to blend.

Add the chickpeas to a large bowl. Using a potato masher, gently smash the beans, leaving some chunky and some whole. Add the tomatoes, shallots, capers and parsley.

Toss with the dressing and mix well to combine. Taste, and adjust seasoning if necessary.

This dish can be served right away at room temperature or chilled up to 3 hours in advance. Enjoy with thick slices of the crusty bread.

# STOVE-TOP MAPLE BAKED BEANS

GLUTEN-FREE

For the record, I absolutely despise baked beans from the can. They taste like...*the can*. Making your own is simple; it's a matter of mixing a few fridge door ingredients with cooked cannellini beans. That's it. To save time, I do this "stove-top" style instead of baking the beans in the oven. From start to finish, it will take about 30–35 minutes. Just do me one favor—use *real* maple syrup for this recipe. No imitation pancake syrup, please!

PS: For extra flavor, I've topped the beans with crispy chards of smoky bacon and flash-fried rosemary leaves.

## SERVES 4–6, AS A SIDE DISH

1 tsp olive oil

4 slices of bacon, cut into 1-inch (2.5-cm) pieces

1 small sprig of rosemary, leaves stripped

1 cup (160 g) diced onions

½ cup (118 ml) ketchup

¼ cup (60 ml) pure maple syrup, plus more to taste

¼ cup (60 ml) Triple-Duty Chicken Stock (page 27) or water

2 tbsp (30 g) Dijon mustard

1 tbsp (15 ml) balsamic vinegar

2 cups (354 g) cooked cannellini beans, rinsed & drained*

Freshly ground black pepper

*For more information on cooking dried cannellini beans, see pages 109–111, or substitute with one 15-ounce (425-g) can of beans.*

In a large, 12-inch (30-cm) skillet, warm the olive oil over low heat. Sauté the bacon until golden, about 3–5 minutes. Add the rosemary leaves to flash fry, about 30 seconds. Transfer the bacon and rosemary to a paper towel–lined plate. Drain the drippings from the pan, reserving about 1 tablespoon (15 ml) to cook the onions.

Sauté the onions until soft, about 3–5 minutes. Pour in the ketchup, maple syrup, chicken stock (or water), Dijon mustard and balsamic vinegar. Bring to a gentle boil, then reduce the heat to low. Simmer gently, stirring occasionally, to reduce the sauce and for the flavors to infuse, about 10–15 minutes.

Add the beans to warm through, about 2–3 minutes. Remove the pan from the heat. Taste and season with a few turns of freshly ground black pepper. Drizzle in extra maple syrup if you'd like it sweeter.

To serve, tip the beans into a casserole dish. Scatter the crispy bacon and rosemary leaves over the top and have a bite!

TIP: If you're out of balsamic vinegar, try apple cider vinegar or red wine vinegar instead.

# TUSCAN WHITE BEAN SOUP, 2 WAYS

This is the most popular soup recipe on my blog. I've updated the original cooking method to include my shortcut for Pre-Chopped Vegetables (page 11) and Triple-Duty Chicken Stock (page 27) to make it come together faster. Infused with bacon and sage, enjoy this Tuscan specialty both ways, creamy or chunky, depending on your mood.

SERVES 4–6

1 tsp olive oil

2 slices of bacon, cut into 1-inch (2.5-cm) pieces

1 cup (160 g) diced onion

½ cup (50 g) diced celery

4 whole sage leaves

2 cloves of garlic, grated

6 cups (1 kg) cooked cannellini beans, rinsed & drained*

1 quart (1 L) Triple-Duty Chicken Stock (page 27), plus more as needed

Coarse salt and freshly ground black pepper

Ground Parmesan cheese, to taste

1 cup (30 g) croutons

Crusty bread for dunking (optional)

*For more information on cooking dried cannellini beans, see pages 109–111, or substitute with three 15-ounce (425-g) cans of beans.*

In a large heavy-bottom pot, warm the olive oil over medium heat. Sauté the bacon until lightly golden, about 5 minutes. Remove the bacon to a paper towel–lined plate.

Add the onion, celery and whole sage leaves to the pan. Sauté until soft, about 5 minutes. Add the garlic and stir until fragrant, 30 seconds. Tilt the pot, and remove most of the residual oil (if any) with a spoon. Add the reserved bacon back to the pan to cook with the rest of the soup. Toss in the beans.

Add the chicken stock and bring the soup to a boil. Reduce the heat to low and simmer (uncovered) for about 15 minutes for the flavors to develop. Season with salt and pepper to taste.

OPTION #1

For chunky soup, simply leave the soup the way it is, adding more stock to get it nice and brothy.

OPTION #2

For creamy soup, purée the soup (including the bacon and sage) using a hand blender, food processor or regular blender. Add additional stock if the soup is too thick.

To serve, divide the soup among bowls and top with Parmesan cheese and croutons. Serve with crusty bread on the side, if using.

TIP: Portion soup into containers and freeze up to 3 months. Defrost for quick weeknight dinners.

# 30-MINUTE WHOLE-GRAIN PASTA WITH WHITE BEANS & TOMATOES

VEGETARIAN

Not all whole-grain pasta tastes like sawdust. Try thin-style angel hair pasta. It has great flavor and cooks up quickly, leaving you just enough time to raid the pantry for the rest of the ingredients used in this dish, including briny olives and capers. I like to make this midweek using up any leftover cannellini beans in the fridge. It's simple, stress-free and comes together in just about 30 minutes.

## SERVES 2 IF YOU'RE STARVING, OR 4 COMFORTABLY

½ lb (227 g) whole-grain angel hair pasta or thin spaghetti

2 tbsp (30 ml) olive oil, plus more for drizzling

2 cups (300 g) cherry tomatoes, whole

2 cloves of garlic, grated

2 cups (354 g) cooked cannellini beans, rinsed & drained*

½ cup (90 g) roughly chopped kalamata olives

1 tbsp (9 g) capers, rinsed

½ cup (30 g) roughly chopped parsley

A few turns of freshly ground black pepper

Wedge of Parmesan cheese, for grating

*For more information on cooking dried cannellini beans, see pages 109–111, or substitute with one 15-ounce (425-g) can of beans.

Bring a pot of water to a boil and cook the pasta according to the package instructions. Drain and set aside. Drizzle with olive oil to prevent sticking.

Meanwhile, in a large, 12-inch (30-cm) skillet, warm the olive oil over medium heat. Add the whole cherry tomatoes and cook until they begin to burst, about 5–6 minutes. Add the garlic and stir until fragrant, about 30 seconds.

To the pan, add the cannellini beans, kalamata olives, capers and chopped parsley.

Add the pasta directly to the pan and toss well with tongs to coat the strands. Alternatively, you can do this in a bowl if you need more room to groove.

To serve, top the pasta with extra olive oil, a few turns of pepper and a generous grating of Parmesan cheese.

# MY FAVORITE BLACK BEAN SOUP

GLUTEN-FREE

Brown food could use a little lipstick, don't you think? In this recipe, you'll find a confetti of colors for both visual *and* flavor appeal. The addition of cherry tomatoes is most welcome, providing a soft sweetness against the subtle crunch of carrots and celery. I've included a few shortcuts to make your life easier as well: Pre-Chopped Vegetables (page 11), homemade Triple-Duty Chicken Stock (page 27) and a dash of Mexican Spice Blend (page 97). *Olé!* Now, if you really want to elevate this soup, try it with pickled jalapeños. Drizzle a spoonful of juice over your soup right before taking a bite. Heaven.

SERVES 4–6

2 tbsp (30 ml) olive oil

1 cup (160 g) diced onions

½ cup (65 g) diced carrots

½ cup (50 g) diced celery

1 clove of garlic, grated

1 tbsp (8 g) Mexican Spice Blend (page 97)

½ tsp cumin

6 cups (1 kg) cooked black beans, rinsed and drained*

4 cups (1 L) Triple-Duty Chicken Stock (page 27), plus more as needed

1 cup (150 g) cherry tomatoes, halved

¼ cup (15 g) roughly chopped cilantro or parsley

Coarse salt and freshly ground black pepper

TOPPINGS

Pickled jalapeños

1 juicy lime, cut into wedges

Handful of cilantro or parsley leaves

*For more information on cooking dried black beans, see pages 109–111, or substitute with four 15-ounce (425-g) cans of beans.*

In a large heavy-bottom pot, warm the olive oil over medium heat. Sauté the onions, carrots and celery until soft, about 3–5 minutes. Add the garlic, Mexican Spice Blend and cumin, and stir until fragrant, 30 seconds. It will smell delicious.

Add the black beans and chicken stock. Bring the soup to a gentle boil and reduce the heat to low. Simmer uncovered for about 20–30 minutes or until the vegetables are tender.

Meanwhile, slice your cherry tomatoes in half. Add them to the pot during the last 10 minutes of cooking to hold their shape.

Purée a small portion of the soup, mostly beans, to give the soup a creamy texture. Use a handheld stick blender if you have one, or do this in your food processor or blender. My preference is to purée about one-third of the soup, for a rustic-style texture.

Stir in your chopped cilantro (or parsley). Taste and season with salt and pepper.

Ladle your soup into bowls and top with pickled jalapeños. Drizzle a spoonful of juice from the jar over your soup for extra flavor. Top with lime wedges and cilantro (or parsley) leaves.

TIP: Try homemade vegetable stock to make this vegetarian- and vegan-friendly.

# SPEEDY SALAD-STUFFED SWEET POTATOES

GLUTEN-FREE — VEGETARIAN

When you're starving, and the thought of cooking makes you roll your eyes and sigh, try these quick stuffed sweet potatoes for dinner. Pop the potatoes into the microwave—they will be ready in less than 10 minutes. Use that time to make a leafy green salad for your stuffing. The natural sweetness of the potatoes will drink in the tangy lime juice, salty feta and protein-packed black beans. It's wonderfully filling.

Feel free to get creative with your greens. Using a combination of mixed baby greens and sprouts will make this sing, but really, use whatever you'd like. I just love sprouts. They're so whimsical and good for you too.

SERVES 4

4 sweet potatoes

4 handfuls of mixed baby greens and sprouts

1 cup (150 g) cherry tomatoes, halved

2 tbsp (30 ml) olive oil

1 tsp fresh lime juice

Coarse salt and freshly ground black pepper

1 cup (172 g) cooked black beans, rinsed & drained*

½ cup (75 g) crumbled feta

Extra lime wedges to serve

*For more information on cooking dried black beans, see pages 109–111, or substitute with approximately three-quarters of a 15-ounce (425-g) can of beans.

Using a fork, prick the sweet potatoes on all sides, about 6 times each. This will allow the steam to escape as they cook. Arrange the sweet potatoes onto a plate and microwave for about 4–8 minutes, rotating at the halfway mark. Quick Tip: Cooking time will vary. To check for doneness, insert a paring knife into the center of each potato; it should release easily. If there's resistance, cook for a few more minutes. Cool for 5 minutes before slicing.

While the potatoes are cooking, make the salad. Add the mixed greens, sprouts and cherry tomatoes to a small bowl. Drizzle with olive oil, squeeze in the lime juice and season lightly with salt and pepper. Toss well.

Using a large knife, slice the potatoes lengthwise about three-quarters of the way down; you don't want to cut them in half, just enough to create a pocket for stuffing.

Spoon ¼ cup (43 g) of black beans into each potato, followed by a good handful of dressed salad. Top with crumbled feta and serve with extra lime wedges on the side.

TIP: Don't have a microwave? Place your pricked sweet potatoes onto a rimmed baking sheet and bake at 425°F (220°C) for about 45 minutes to 1 hour, depending on size.

# ONE-POT CARIBBEAN BLACK BEANS & COUSCOUS

Okay, so I already told you about my love affair with black beans and rice with avocados. This one-pot meal is a riff on the classic, only faster. It begins with a quick sauté of aromatics, including sweet onions and peppers followed by a can of fire-roasted tomatoes. The couscous will quickly absorb the delicious flavors, becoming light and fluffy in about 15–20 minutes. Don't forget the creamy avocado on top—it's the best part!

SERVES 4–6

2 tbsp (30 ml) olive oil, plus more for serving

1 cup (160 g) diced onion

1 green bell pepper, diced

Coarse salt and freshly ground black pepper

2 cloves of garlic, grated

1 (14-oz [397-g]) can of fire-roasted diced tomatoes

3 cups (500 g) cooked black beans, rinsed and drained*

1 cup (175 g) whole-grain couscous, dry

1 cup (237 ml) Triple-Duty Chicken Stock (page 27)

¼ cup (15 g) roughly chopped cilantro or parsley

1–2 Hass avocados

2 juicy limes, cut into wedges

*For more information on cooking dried black beans, see pages 109–111, or substitute with two 15-ounce (425-g) cans of beans.

In a large pot, warm the olive oil over medium heat. Sauté the onion and pepper to soften, about 5–7 minutes. Season with salt and pepper. Add the grated garlic and stir until fragrant, about 30 seconds.

To the pot, add the fire-roasted tomatoes, black beans and couscous. Pour in the stock and bring to a boil. Place the lid on top, and remove the pot from the heat. Let the couscous sit for about 15–20 minutes for the liquid to absorb. Quick Tip: To check if it's ready, gently rake a fork through your couscous; it should be light and fluffy. If there's more liquid to be absorbed, just pop the lid back on and wait a couple of minutes.

To serve, drizzle extra olive oil over the couscous to give it a glossy sheen. Toss in the chopped cilantro (or parsley) and mix well. Portion into bowls. Dice up your avocado and add to each bowl. Squeeze some lime juice over the top with extra lime wedges ready to go on the side.

TIP: Try homemade vegetable stock for a delicious vegetarian or vegan version.

# chapter six

# PROCESS THIS

Ever fall victim to one of those late-night infomercials?

You know, the ones that persuade you to buy their latest and greatest kitchen appliance that "does it all"?

Oh, yes. Been there. You get suckered in, only to use your shiny new toy once or twice to make a smoothie. Nowadays, for an appliance to even qualify in my kitchen it needs to be accessible both literally and figuratively. If it's buried under decades of kitchen clutter, I'll never use it. And if it's too intimidating to even operate, forget about it.

Enter the food processor.

For the longest time, I only used my late-night purchase to purée soup and make baby food. I didn't know what else to do with it, quite frankly. It wasn't until I had kids and limited time, that I was forced to dig out this beast for culinary assistance. The food processor helped me do everything quickly: slice vegetables, shred cheese, make muffins (before school!). There was potential. I just had to find it.

At the time of writing this book, my food processor is about 10 years old. Obviously, it's not the latest and greatest model equipped with e-mail capabilities and social media access, but rather slightly vintage and dusted in flour. But it gets the job done. In this chapter, you'll learn how to make several easy recipes, including my flaky No-Roll Blueberry Scones (page 141), No-Peel Butternut Squash Soup (page 133) and the almighty Banana Cloud Cake (page 142). For the sake of convenience, keep your food processor easily accessible and take advantage of your dishwasher (human or otherwise) to clean the bowl and blades.

If you don't have a food processor, no worries—you can still make the recipes in this section. But if you do have one, life in the kitchen will be that much easier. It's prep work simplified.

# NO-PEEL BUTTERNUT SQUASH SOUP

GLUTEN-FREE

I have many nemeses in the culinary world. Mashed potatoes? Won't do it. Grating cheese? Pass. Peeling squash? I've always relied on my vegetable peeler to strip the leathery skin from butternut squash. Now, I use the food processor instead. Run the squash through the machine to create beautiful thin slices that will not only cook faster, there's no need to peel! The outer skin becomes incredibly soft (and edible) when cooked. Using Pre-Chopped Vegetables (page 11) will make your life easier too.

The flavor of this soup is naturally sweet from the squash with subtle hints of smokiness from the bacon. Right before serving, swirl a little half and half over the top for luscious, creamy flavor.

## SERVES 4

1 tsp olive oil

2 slices of bacon, cut into 1-inch (2.5-cm) pieces

2 cups (320 g) diced onion

½ cup (65 g) diced carrot

½ cup (50 g) diced celery

8 cups (1 kg) sliced butternut squash, skin on

4 cups (1 L) Triple-Duty Chicken Stock (page 27), plus more as needed

Coarse salt and freshly ground black pepper

Swirl of half and half or cream (optional)

Grab a large heavy-bottom pot and warm the olive oil over medium heat. Sauté the bacon, stirring occasionally, until golden brown, about 5 minutes. Keep the bacon in the pot.

Add the onion, carrots and celery. Continue to sauté for about 10 minutes. You're looking for a nice, golden color on the veggies.

While that's going, fit your food processor with the slicer attachment. Slice the butternut squash in half lengthwise and scrape out the seeds. Cut the squash to fit the mouth of the feed tube. Process through the machine for thin slices. Quick Tip: Depending on the size of your squash you might end up with more than you need; reserve 8 cups (1 kg) for the soup and freeze the rest.

Add the squash to the pot and pour in the chicken stock. Place the lid on top and bring to a boil. Reduce the heat and simmer (covered) for about 20–30 minutes, or until the vegetables are tender.

In the meantime, quickly rinse out your food processor. Fit the bowl with the blade attachment. You will use this to purée the soup.

Working in batches, purée the soup until smooth. Always use caution when blending hot liquids; wait until slightly cooled if necessary. Add more stock as needed if it becomes too thick. Return the soup to the pot and season with salt and pepper. Add a swirl of half and half (or cream) to taste. Soup's on!

TIP: Portion this soup into containers and freeze up to 3 months. Defrost for quick weeknight dinners.

# NO-ROLL TURKEY MEATBALLS WITH SPINACH & RAISINS

Meatballs are classic comfort food. My version is not only easy to prepare, it's conveniently baked in the oven, not fried. The food processor eliminates chopping and lightens the overall texture. And there's no need to roll; use a mini ice cream scoop to easily portion the meatballs straight onto the baking sheet. This way, if the phone rings, you won't have raw meat all over your hands.

The addition of raisins might sound like an unusual ingredient, but the subtle sweetness is delicious. It's very Sicilian. I learned this trick from my grandmother.

## SERVES 6–8

1 tbsp (15 ml) olive oil

1 bunch of scallions, thinly sliced, white and light green part only

1 (4-oz [113-g]) bag baby spinach

¼ cup (36 g) raisins (optional)

1 lb (454 g) ground turkey or chicken, white and dark meat mix for best flavor

1 extra large egg

¾ cup (90 g) Italian seasoned breadcrumbs

Coarse salt and freshly ground black pepper

### TO SERVE

4 cups (946 ml) Basic Tomato Sauce (page 40)

Pasta, whole-grains or good bread for sandwiches (optional)

Preheat your oven to 350°F (175°C). Grab two rimmed baking sheets and line with parchment paper.

In a large, 12-inch (30-cm) skillet, warm the olive oil over low heat. Add the scallions and sauté, without coloring, until soft, about 1 minute. Toss in the spinach and raisins, and cook until the leaves begin to wilt, about 1 minute. Transfer the vegetables to the food processor.

Pulse your veggies about 2–3 times to lightly chop. Add the ground turkey (or chicken), egg and breadcrumbs. Season with salt and a few grinds of black pepper. Continue to pulse until the mixture is well combined. Unplug the food processor and remove the bowl from the base.

Using a mini ice cream scoop, about 1 inch (1.3 cm) in diameter, portion the meatballs onto your prepared baking sheets. Bake in the center of the oven for about 25 minutes, turning them over at the 15-minute mark, so that both sides brown evenly.

Meanwhile, get a pot going to warm up your tomato sauce. When the meatballs are ready, toss them into the sauce to soak up the delicious tomato flavor.

Serve with pasta, whole-grains or make sandwiches—your choice.

TIP: Double or triple this recipe and freeze, up to 3 months. Defrost for quick weeknight dinners.

# SIMPLE RADISH & AVOCADO SALAD

GLUTEN-FREE — VEGETARIAN — VEGAN

Most people don't realize that radishes are a 2-for-1 deal; the leaves are perfectly edible. All they need is a good rinse under cold water and you've got instant salad greens. For the radishes themselves, I like to slice them paper thin, almost see through. This can be difficult to do by hand (hello, they're round) so toss them into your food processor for instant, thin slices. Crunchy radishes pair well with cool and creamy avocados.

SERVES 2

BALSAMIC JAM JAR VINAIGRETTE

1 tbsp (15 ml) balsamic vinegar

¼ cup (60 ml) red wine vinegar

½ cup (118 ml) olive oil

Coarse salt and freshly ground black pepper

1 bunch of small radishes with their leafy green tops

1 ripe Hass avocado

To make the dressing, add the first three ingredients to an empty jam jar. Season with salt and pepper. Screw the lid on tight and shake well to blend.

Separate the radishes from their leafy green tops. Rinse and dry thoroughly in a salad spinner. Gently tear the leaves into bite-size pieces and add to a salad bowl.

To thinly slice the radishes, fit your food processor with the slicer attachment. Run the radishes through the machine. Quick Tip: If your radishes are large, slice them in half first before processing; you'll have lovely half-moon shapes. Add the radishes to the salad bowl.

Drizzle the vinaigrette over the salad. When you're ready to eat, dice up your avocado and toss gently to combine.

TIP: One bunch of radishes will typically yield enough leaves for a small salad. To stretch it out, toss in additional handfuls of baby greens such as mesclun or spinach to feed a crowd.

# CAULIFLOWER BOLOGNESE

VEGETARIAN

My grandfather used to braise cauliflower in tomato sauce and serve it with pasta. As a kid, I thought this was beyond weird, but I ate it anyway because it was actually really good. Cauliflower adds a wonderful flavor to the sauce.

For this recipe, I blitz up the cauliflower to mimic ground beef. Chopping cauliflower by hand is very messy, so you're going to love that it's done in the food processor. Another clever shortcut is the addition of red lentils. The lentils not only add a boost of protein, they also act as a natural thickener, giving the sauce great texture without having to babysit the stove waiting for the sauce to thicken.

SERVES 4–6

1 small head of cauliflower

2 tbsp (30 g) unsalted butter

1 cup (160 g) diced onions

1 garlic clove, grated

2 (28-oz [794-g]) cans of whole plum tomatoes in thick purée

½ cup (96 g) red lentils

Coarse salt and freshly ground black pepper

1 lb (454 g) thin spaghetti

Drizzle of olive oil

Handful of fresh basil leaves

Wedge of Parmesan cheese, for grating

Slice the cauliflower in half, removing the thick center core. Cut into large chunks.

To a food processor, break up the cauliflower into florets. Do not dump all of the cauliflower at once. You'll need to process in batches to create uniform pieces.

Pulse the cauliflower, only 1–2 times. It will look crumbly with small florets throughout—this is perfect. Dump the mixture into a large bowl and repeat this step until you've processed all of the cauliflower.

In a large heavy-bottomed pot, warm the butter over low heat. Add the onions and sauté until soft, about 3–5 minutes.

Add the cauliflower to the pot. Increase the heat to medium and continue to cook, stirring occasionally, until the cauliflower begins to lose its shape and takes on a light golden color, about 5–6 minutes. Grate in the garlic and cook until fragrant, about 30 seconds.

Pour in the tomatoes and red lentils. Mix until well combined.

Place the lid on top and bring the sauce to a gentle boil. Reduce the heat to low and simmer (covered), for about 30 minutes. Remove the lid and cook for an additional 15 minutes or so, until the cauliflower is tender and the lentils are broken down. The sauce should look thickened. Season with salt and pepper to taste.

When you're about ready to eat, bring a pot of water to a boil. Cook the pasta according to the package instructions. Drain and return to the pot. Drizzle with olive oil to coat.

Portion your hearty cauliflower sauce over the pasta and top with basil leaves and freshly grated Parmesan cheese, to serve.

# NO-ROLL BLUEBERRY SCONES

VEGETARIAN

This shortcut, no-roll method is fantastic. Traditional scones require several steps: cutting the butter into the flour, kneading the dough and then rolling it out into shapes. Skip all of that. Use your food processor to blend the butter directly into the dry ingredients, and instead of rolling out the dough, simply scoop the rubbly mixture onto your baking tray using a ¼-cup (60-ml) measure. You'll end up with the best light and flaky scones. These are studded with juicy blueberries that burst in the oven when baked. Beautiful.

Perhaps, a pat of Cinnamon Sugar Butter (page 75) might interest you?

MAKES 8–10 SCONES

DRY

2 cups (250 g) flour

⅓ cup (66 g) sugar

2 tsp (9 g) baking powder

½ tsp baking soda

Pinch of salt

8 tbsp (120 g) unsalted butter, cut into ½-inch (1.3-cm) cubes, cold

WET

1 extra large egg

¼ cup (50 g) Greek yogurt

¼ cup (60 ml) milk

1 tsp pure vanilla extract

1 cup (150 g) fresh or frozen blueberries

Cinnamon Sugar Butter (page 75), for serving (optional)

Preheat your oven to 400°F (200°C). Line a rimmed baking sheet with parchment paper.

To a food processor, add all of your dry ingredients except the butter. Run the machine to combine. Toss in the butter cubes and pulse, about 8–10 times, until small "crumbs" start to form.

In a separate large bowl, whisk the wet ingredients together.

Combine the dry and wet ingredients in one bowl, and fold in the blueberries. Gently mix the dough until it comes together (not into a ball).

Using a ¼-cup (60-ml) measure, scoop the dough out onto your prepared baking sheet about 2 inches (5 cm) apart.

Bake for about 25–30 minutes, or until golden brown.

Remove the scones from the oven and cool for 5 minutes on the tray. Transfer to a wire rack to finish cooling.

Serve warm or at room temperature with a pat of cinnamon sugar butter, if desired, and a strong cup of coffee or tea.

# BANANA CLOUD CAKE

VEGETARIAN

One of my biggest gripes with making banana bread is having to mash the bananas with a fork. It's typical procedure for this sort of recipe but for whatever reason, I can't get it right—the bananas stick and glob to the bottom of the bowl. A quick blitz in the food processor solves this problem and subsequently, incorporates air into the mix making the crumb light as a cloud. What a great, unexpected discovery.

Also, this cake won't taste anywhere near its full potential with *pale yellow* bananas. Choose overripe bananas, speckled heavily with brown spots for best flavor. Don't cheat.

## MAKES 12 SNACK SQUARES

### DRY

1¼ cups (156 g) flour

1 tsp baking powder

½ baking soda

½ tsp salt

1 tsp cinnamon

Dash of nutmeg

### WET

2 very ripe, brown-speckled bananas

2 eggs

⅓ cup (78 ml) oil

½ cup (100 g) sugar

1½ tsp (7 ml) vanilla

### NUT TOPPING

1 heaped cup (117 g) walnuts, roughly chopped

Powdered sugar, for dusting

Preheat your oven to 350°F (175°C). Line an 8 x 8-inch (20 x 20-cm) square pan with parchment paper, leaving excess paper to hang over the sides for easy removal.

In a large bowl, add the dry ingredients and whisk well to blend.

To a food processor, add all of your wet ingredients. Run the machine until the bananas are creamy and smooth.

Add the dry ingredients (don't dump) evenly around the bowl. Pulse in quick, short bursts, *only 2–3 times.* That's it! Quick Tip: Resist the urge to over-pulse; the mixture will toughen up and become dry when baked. That is definitely not cloud-like....

Pour the batter into your lined pan, scraping down the sides of the bowl with a rubber spatula. Scatter the chopped walnuts over the top.

Bake in the oven, center rack, for about 25–30 minutes, or until a toothpick comes out clean when inserted. The cake will look beautifully puffed and golden, and it will smell wonderful.

Cool the cake in the pan for about 10 minutes. Then, using your parchment-paper handles, transfer the cake to a wire rack to finish cooling. Dust with powdered sugar to finish, and enjoy your slice (or square) of heaven.

TIP: Try this cake with a sprinkle of Convenient Crumbles (page 79) over the top for extra cinnamon buttery goodness.

# 3-INGREDIENT FROZEN YOGURT

GLUTEN-FREE — VEGETARIAN

This healthy sweet treat rivals rich, decadent gelato. And there are only three ingredients! Okay, possibly four if you count the (optional) honey. But here's the best part: The whole blending business is done right in the food processor. There's no need for an ice cream machine or lengthy freezing time overnight. It's practically instant.

To really enjoy its soft, velvety texture, make your frozen yogurt right before serving. It only takes two minutes.

## SERVES 4

1 cup (150 g) frozen strawberries

1 cup (150 g) frozen sliced bananas

1 cup (200 g) Greek yogurt

Honey (optional)

To a food processor, add the strawberries and bananas. Pulse several times until the fruit is broken up.

With the machine running, add the Greek yogurt. Continue to process until smooth. Drizzle in the honey to taste, if using. Quick Tip: Do not run the machine for too long; the heat from the blade will melt the frozen fruit. If this happens, no worries. Just pop the yogurt into the freezer for a couple of minutes to firm up.

To serve, scoop your frozen yogurt into bowls, ice cream cones or just dig in with a spoon! Store leftovers in an airtight container and freeze.

TIP: Feel free to switch up the frozen fruit as desired (a combination of mango and banana is delicious). Just keep the ratio of fruit to yogurt 2:1 for best results.

*chapter seven*

# BATCH-COOKED GRAINS

Once upon a time, I made quinoa-crumbed chicken cutlets and vowed never to do it again.

There were too many steps involved: cooking the quinoa, cooling the quinoa, dredging the chicken in flour, egg, quinoa...*the cleanup*! By the time I was finished, the kitchen was destroyed, I was sweating and there was more quinoa on my floor than on the actual chicken itself. Major fail.

Now I batch-cook my grains.

This strategy is a practical, time-saving solution for when recipes call for cooked and cooled grains. I can't even tell you how many times I've pulled out a container of leftover brown rice and thrown together a simple side dish with lemon and olive oil—in less than 10 minutes! It's a great get-ahead tip for my Easy Quinoa Chicken with Apricot Yogurt Sauce (page 165) too. Keep a stash of cooked grains in your fridge or freezer and you will always be ready for amazing meals in a matter of minutes.

This sections highlights how to batch-cook grains, specifically fluffy basmati rice, quinoa and short-grain brown rice. The recipes are flexible, so feel free to use whatever combination of grains you like—it's all good.

# YOUR GRAIN GUIDE

In this chapter, you'll learn how to prepare three common varieties of grains: basmati rice, quinoa and short-grain brown rice. While the initial preparation is similar, cooking time will vary according to grain.

## RINSE

Rinse your grains thoroughly under cold water. This will remove any impurities, grit and bitterness, especially found in quinoa.

## COOK

Add your specified amount of water and a pinch of salt to a large pot, then bring to a boil. Add the grains and place the lid on top. Reduce the heat to low and simmer, without stirring, until tender (use the chart below for estimated cooking time). Once your grains are done, remove the lid and set aside; this will allow the moisture to evaporate, leaving your grains light and fluffy. Rake gently with a fork to separate.

> TIP: For extra flavor, cook your grains in Triple-Duty Chicken Stock (page 27) or vegetable stock.

### Cooking Times for Grains

| 1 CUP DRIED GRAINS | WATER OR STOCK | COOKING TIME | YIELD |
|---|---|---|---|
| White Basmati Rice (185 g) | 1½ cups (355 ml) | 15–20 minutes | 3 cups (480 g) |
| Quinoa (any color) (170 g) | 2 cups (473 ml) | 15–20 minutes | 4 cups (740 g) |
| Short-Grain Brown Rice (190 g) | 1¾ cups (414 ml) | 45–50 minutes | 3–4 cups (585–780 g) |

## STORAGE

Spread the grains out on a rimmed baking sheet and allow to cool at room temperature before storing. Or, if you're in a hurry, place the baking sheet into the fridge (space permitting) to speed things up.

Once cooled, transfer to airtight containers or zip-top bags and label and date, respectively.

Refrigerate up to 1 week, or freeze 1 to 3 months. Defrost in the microwave or submerge into a bowl of cold water to thaw.

# 3-CHEESE STUFFED PEPPERS

**GLUTEN-FREE**

Stuffed peppers make an excellent weeknight dinner. The beauty of using precooked rice is that you can prep everything in advance and simply bake when ready to serve. These are wonderful for entertaining.

## SERVES 4 HUNGRY PEOPLE, OR 6 WITH SALAD ON THE SIDE

1 tbsp (15 ml) olive oil

1 tbsp (15 g) unsalted butter

10 oz (284 g) baby portobello mushrooms

1 (4-oz [113-g]) bag of baby spinach

2 garlic cloves, grated

Coarse salt and freshly ground black pepper

4 sweet bell peppers, assorted colors

2 cups (320 g) cooked basmati rice, room temperature or cold*

¼ cup (60 ml) Triple-Duty Chicken Stock (page 27)

¼ cup (25 g) ground Parmesan cheese, plus more to taste

½ cup (135 g) crumbled goat cheese

2 cups (200 g) grated fontina cheese, divided

*Approximately ¾ cup (135 g) dry basmati rice yields 2 cups (320 g) cooked. For more information on cooking rice, see page 149.*

Preheat your oven to 350°F (175°C). Find a baking dish to fit your peppers snuggly and line with parchment paper for easy cleanup.

In a large, 12-inch (30-cm) skillet, melt the olive oil and butter over medium heat. Tear up the mushrooms directly into the pan. It's faster than slicing and it's one less thing to chop. Sauté until golden and all of the moisture has evaporated, about 5 minutes. Reduce the heat to low.

To the pan, add your spinach one handful at a time and toss gently to wilt. Add the garlic and cook for 30 seconds. Season with salt and pepper. Transfer the filling to a bowl to cool.

To prepare the peppers, slice them in half lengthwise through the stem. Remove and discard the seeds and any rib pieces. You should have 8 hollow cups.

To your filling, add the rice, chicken stock and Parmesan cheese. Mix well. Gently fold in the goat cheese and 1 cup (100 g) of fontina cheese.

Stuff each pepper with a portion of the filling and place into your baking dish. Cover with foil and bake for about 30–35 minutes. The peppers should be soft but still hold their shape when ready.

To finish, top the peppers with the remaining 1 cup (100 g) of fontina cheese and an extra sprinkle of Parmesan. Broil on low uncovered, until the cheese is bubbly and melted, 2–3 minutes.

Allow to cool for 1–2 minutes before serving.

TIP: Substitute with vegetable stock for a flavorful vegetarian version.

# ASPARAGUS & GOAT CHEESE FRITTATA WITH A CRISPY RICE CRUST

GLUTEN-FREE — VEGETARIAN

Remember this formula: 6 eggs + 2 cups (320 g) leftover grains + 1 cup (134 g) veggies.

If you have these ingredients, you can make this frittata anytime you want—it's flexible. For the crust, leftover basmati rice is layered at the bottom of the skillet before the egg and asparagus filling is poured on top. It forms a golden, crunchy crust when baked.

Serve warm or at room temperature.

## SERVES 4 FOR DINNER, OR 6 AS A LIGHT BITE

6 extra large eggs

½ cup (100 g) plain Greek yogurt

1 cup (134 g) sliced asparagus, cut on a diagonal about ½ inch (1.3 cm) thick, tips reserved

Coarse salt and freshly ground black pepper

1 tbsp (15 ml) olive oil

1 tbsp (15 g) unsalted butter

2 cups (320 g) cooked basmati rice, room temperature or cold*

¼ cup (25 g) thinly sliced scallions, white and light green part only

½ cup (136 g) crumbled goat cheese

*Approximately ¾ cup (135 g) dry basmati rice yields 2 cups (320 g) cooked. For more information on cooking rice, see page 149.*

Adjust your oven racks to fit the top third portion of the oven. Preheat to 425°F (220°C).

For the filling, whisk the eggs and Greek yogurt in a large bowl. The mixture might look curdled at first, but will eventually blend together. Add the sliced asparagus and season with salt and pepper.

In a large, 10-inch (25-cm) cast-iron skillet, warm the olive oil and butter over low heat. Add the rice and stir well to coat the grains, about 30 seconds. Season lightly with salt and pepper. Using the back of a wooden spoon, spread out the grains on the bottom of your skillet; this is your crust. Sprinkle the scallions over the top.

Pour the egg filling into the skillet, tilting the pan to spread the filling all the way around. Decorate with the reserved asparagus tips and goat cheese.

Bake in the oven, top rack, until the filling is set and the top golden brown, about 30 minutes. Cool for 5 minutes before slicing.

TIP: When choosing asparagus, go for the medium-fat stalks. They have better flavor and can withstand 30 minutes in a hot oven while holding their shape. The skinny asparagus will cook too quickly in this frittata and get mushy.

# CASHEW FRIED RICE

GLUTEN-FREE OPTION — VEGETARIAN

*Cold, day-old rice*...is the secret to excellent fried rice. If your rice is too hot it won't fry properly; it turns to mush. Using leftover rice or any grain for that matter is the perfect solution. You could even add chicken, shrimp or pork to morph this into a substantial meal for dinner.

Mung bean sprouts add wonderful crunch to this dish, but if you can't find any (just ask—most markets carry them) simply leave them out.

## SERVES 2 AS A SIDE DISH

3 tbsp (45 ml) vegetable oil, divided

½ red bell pepper, roughly chopped

1 handful of snow peas, roughly chopped

2 cups (320 g) cooked basmati rice, room temperature or cold*

1 clove of garlic, grated

4 tsp (20 ml) soy sauce (or tamari for gluten-free)

½ tsp sugar

1 handful of mung bean sprouts

½ cup (67 g) frozen peas

¼ cup (25 g) sliced scallions, white and light green part only

½ cup (113 g) chopped cashews

1 tbsp (4 g) roughly chopped parsley

1 juicy lime (optional)

*Approximately ¾ cup (135 g) dry basmati rice yields 2 cups (320 g) cooked. For more information on cooking rice, see page 149.*

In a large, 10-inch (25-cm) cast-iron skillet, warm 2 tablespoons (30 ml) of vegetable oil over medium-high heat. Sauté the peppers until lightly caramelized, about 4–5 minutes. Add the snow peas and cook about 1 minute. Lower the heat.

Pour in the remaining 1 tablespoon (15 ml) of vegetable oil. Add the rice and stir well to coat the grains. Quick Tip: If your rice is particularly cold or stuck together, mash it with a fork to break up the grains.

Grate the garlic into the pan, then add the soy sauce (or tamari) and sugar. Stir constantly until the rice takes on a golden brown color. Add the mung beans spouts and frozen peas. Continue to cook until the sprouts are lightly wilted.

Taste the rice, adding more soy sauce and sugar to your liking. It's a balancing act of sweet and salty flavors.

When ready to eat, top with scallions, cashews and parsley. Squeeze in some lime juice, if you're in the mood, and serve.

# EASY ZUCCHINI & BROWN RICE GRATIN

VEGETARIAN

As much as I love brown rice, particularly the short-grain variety, it takes forever to cook—almost 45 minutes! Using precooked rice is a brilliant time-saving shortcut. The grains are layered with thinly sliced zucchini, sweet onions and topped with juicy cherry tomatoes. And the best part? The crunchy Parmesan and breadcrumb topping!

I should also mention, this is not your traditional gratin laden with cream. Instead, I've tucked super-melty fontina cheese into the rice for a unique boost of creamy flavor.

## SERVES 4–6

1 tbsp (15 g) unsalted butter, plus more for coating baking dish

1 tbsp (15 ml) olive oil

½ cup (80 g) diced onion

2 cups (226 g) thinly sliced zucchini about ¼-inch (6-mm) thick (1–2 medium zucchini)

Coarse salt and freshly ground black pepper

3 cups (585 g) cooked short-grain brown rice, room temperature or cold*

1½ cups (162 g) grated fontina cheese

1 cup (150 g) cherry tomatoes, halved

### PARMESAN & BREADCRUMB TOPPING

2 tbsp (10 g) ground Parmesan cheese

2 tbsp (15 g) Italian seasoned breadcrumbs

Drizzle of olive oil

*Approximately 1 cup (190 g) dry short-grain brown rice yields 3–4 cups (585–780 g) cooked. For more information on cooking rice, see page 149.

Adjust your oven racks to fit the top third portion of the oven. Preheat to 425°F (220°C).

Grab a 9 x 13-inch (23 x 33-cm) baking dish and lightly coat with butter.

In a large nonstick skillet, melt the butter and olive oil over medium heat. Sauté the onions until soft and translucent, about 3 minutes. Add the zucchini and cook for about 1 minute; it will finish cooking in the oven. Season with salt and pepper. Remove the pan from the heat.

Working directly in your baking dish, mix the rice and fontina cheese together (I do this with my hands). Make sure the fontina is evenly distributed so you get oozy, melty cheese in every bite. Smooth the mixture with the back of a spoon to fit the dish nicely.

Top the rice with the sautéed zucchini and onions. Wedge in your cherry tomatoes.

For the topping, add the Parmesan cheese and breadcrumbs to a small bowl. Drizzle with olive oil and mix to combine. Sprinkle over the top of the gratin.

Bake for about 15 minutes to warm the rice. Broil for 1–2 minutes to brown the crust.

Cool for 1–2 minutes before diving in.

# 3-MINUTE TROPICAL BREAKFAST BOWL

GLUTEN-FREE — VEGETARIAN — VEGAN

Step aside, oatmeal. You've been outdone. This breakfast bowl offers a broad spectrum of nutrients, including fiber, vitamins and minerals. And it's quick: Simply combine leftover short-grain brown rice with a touch of coconut milk and simmer until warm. It's ready in about three minutes.

You can sweeten these grains with maple syrup, but I find that thick slices of ripe banana and peaches do the trick. It's a delicious way to start the day.

## SERVES 1

1 cup (195 g) cooked short-grain brown rice*

½ cup (118 ml) coconut milk

½ banana, sliced

1 small peach or nectarine, sliced

Maple syrup, to taste

*Approximately ¼ cup (50 g) dry short-grain brown rice yields 1 cup (195 g) cooked. For more information on cooking rice, see page 149.

In a small pot, combine the brown rice and coconut milk. Warm over low heat, about 2–3 minutes. The mixture should be nice and creamy.

To serve, add to a shallow bowl and top with banana and peach slices. Add a touch of maple syrup, to taste.

TIP: As a variation, try this breakfast bowl with quinoa for extra protein. Freeze any leftover fruit and blend with coconut milk for smoothies throughout the week.

# WEEKNIGHT LEMON BROWN RICE

GLUTEN-FREE — VEGETARIAN — VEGAN

You can't mess this up. Mixing precooked brown rice with good-quality olive oil, tangy lemon juice and punchy scallions is a quick and easy side dish. It's delicious with my Sheet Pan Honey-Mustard-Glazed Salmon (page 175). Plus, it's ready in about 10 minutes.

## SERVES 4, AS A SIDE DISH

2 tbsp (30 ml) olive oil, plus extra for drizzling

2 scallions, thinly sliced, white and light green part only

Zest and juice of 1 lemon, divided

3 cups (585 g) cooked short-grain brown rice, room temperature or cold*

Coarse salt and freshly ground black pepper

*Approximately 1 cup (190 g) dry short-grain brown rice yields 3–4 cups (585–780 g) cooked. For more information on cooking rice, see page 149.

In a large nonstick skillet, warm the olive oil over low heat. Add the scallions and stir until fragrant, about 30 seconds. Add the lemon zest and juice of ½ lemon— reserve the other half to squeeze in at the end.

Add the brown rice into the pan and stir to warm through. This should take about 3–4 minutes. Season with salt and pepper to taste.

To serve, pile your rice into a large bowl and drizzle with extra olive oil. Add extra lemon juice from the remaining ½ lemon, if you'd like.

TIP: If you're out of scallions, try grating in half a garlic clove for flavor. This recipe works with basmati rice and quinoa as well.

# SOUTHWESTERN QUINOA SALAD

GLUTEN-FREE — VEGETARIAN

This recipe was conceived at a red light. I was starving, wondering what the car in front of me was going to have for lunch. I was wondering what *I* was going to have for lunch (see what happens when you skip breakfast?). At home, there was quinoa in the freezer, which is perfect for quick throw-together salads; it's one less step to prep. Tossed with colorful veggies and a lip-smacking vinaigrette, the flavor combination is vibrant and fresh. If someone asked me to bring a side dish to a gathering, I'd show up with this.

PS: Try adding creamy avocado, sliced cucumbers and goat cheese for variety.

SERVES 4

3 cups (555 g) cooked quinoa, room temperature*

1½ cups (258 g) cooked black beans, rinsed and drained**

1 cup (164 g) corn kernels, leftover fresh, frozen or canned

1 cup (150 g) cherry tomatoes, halved

½ cup (75 g) finely diced orange bell pepper

¼ cup (25 g) scallions, thinly sliced, white and light green part only

½ cup (30 g) chopped cilantro or parsley, reserving a few sprigs for garnish

### HONEY-LIME JAM JAR DRESSING

¼ cup (60 ml) fresh lime juice

2 tbsp (30 ml) balsamic vinegar

1 tbsp (21 g) honey

1 tsp cumin

½ cup (118 ml) olive oil

Coarse salt and freshly ground black pepper

To a large bowl, add the quinoa, black beans, corn, cherry tomatoes, bell pepper, scallions and cilantro (or parsley). Toss well to combine. Quick Tip: If using frozen corn, quickly thaw prior to using.

For the dressing, add the first five ingredients to an empty jam jar. Season with salt and pepper. Screw the lid on tight and shake well to blend (make sure the honey is completely dissolved). Save any leftover dressing for salads during the week.

Lightly drizzle some of the vinaigrette over the salad and mix it together. Taste, and adjust seasoning if necessary. Top with cilantro (or parsley) springs.

This salad tastes best after it has had a chance to sit for about ½ hour. However, if you're starving or if you've been picking at it with a fork this entire time, go ahead and eat!

TIP: To get ahead, you can make this salad up to 3 hours in advance, dressed lightly. Add extra herbs and more vinaigrette right before serving to refresh the flavors.

*Approximately ¾ cup (125 g) dry quinoa yields 3 cups (555 g) cooked. For more information on cooking quinoa, see page 149.*

**For more information on cooking dried black beans, see pages 109–111, or substitute with one 15-ounce (425-g) can of beans.*

# EASY QUINOA CHICKEN WITH APRICOT YOGURT SAUCE

Quinoa-crumbed *anything* used to be the bane of my existence. Using quinoa straight out of the pot just doesn't work; it's too sticky. Cooked and *cold* is definitely the way to go. The texture is dry, which allows the grains to adhere to the chicken with less of a struggle. And the whole breading business is done in large zip-top bags for easy cleanup. Now, don't get me wrong, it's still a little messy. But if you have leftover quinoa in the fridge (or freezer), now is your chance to experiment.

PS: Chicken tenders instead of chicken breasts are preferred for this recipe. They are naturally juicy and can withstand roasting for 20–25 minutes without getting dry.

## SERVES 4

Cooking spray

1 extra large egg

Splash of water

¼ cup (31 g) flour

2½ cups (460 g) cooked quinoa, cold*

¼ cup (25 g) ground Parmesan cheese

¼ cup (30 g) Italian seasoned breadcrumbs

Coarse salt and freshly ground black pepper

1¼ lbs (567 g) chicken tenders

**APRICOT YOGURT SAUCE**

¼ cup (50 g) Greek yogurt

¼ cup (60 ml) mayonnaise

¼ cup (80 g) apricot jam

1 tsp Dijon mustard

1 lemon, cut into wedges (optional)

*Approximately ⅔ cup (115 g) dry quinoa yields 2½ cups (460 g), cooked. For more information on cooking quinoa, see page 149.*

Adjust your baking rack to fit the top third of the oven. Preheat to 400°F (200°C). Grab a rimmed baking sheet and line with parchment paper. Coat the tray with cooking spray—this helps to brown the underside of the chicken.

In a large bowl, crack the egg and beat well with a splash of water. This is your egg wash.

For your breading station, get yourself 2 large zip-top bags. Add the flour to one bag. In the other bag, add the quinoa, Parmesan cheese, breadcrumbs and a good pinch of salt and pepper. Mix with a fork to combine. Add the chicken tenders to the flour and shake well to coat.

Working in batches, dunk the chicken into the egg wash shaking off any excess as you go. Then press the chicken into your quinoa mixture to coat. Place onto your lined baking sheet. Repeat this process until all of the chicken has been coated.

Generously spray each chicken tender with cooking spray. When you think it's well coated, spray more. This will ensure a nice golden crust.

Bake on the top rack for about 20–25 minutes.

Meanwhile, add the apricot yogurt sauce ingredients into a small bowl. Whisk well to combine. Set aside until ready to serve.

Remove the chicken from the oven and serve with your sweet and tangy apricot sauce for dunking and lemon wedges, if using, for a burst of citrus flavor.

TIP: As a variation, top the quinoa chicken with balsamic-dressed greens, cherry tomatoes and fresh mozzarella.

# CHOCOLATE PEANUT BUTTER & QUINOA TRUFFLES

GLUTEN-FREE — VEGETARIAN

Quinoa in truffles? It might sound strange, but when blended into the peanut butter filling, quinoa helps to bind the ingredients together and disappears both in appearance and flavor. You'll end up with a rich and creamy center, just like a real truffle (but better for you).

And don't bother rolling them yourself—use a mini ice cream scoop to quickly portion the truffles into mini chocolate chips for a crunchy outside shell. It's a clever way to use up that last bit of quinoa you might have in the back of the fridge.

PS: Mini chocolate morsels are preferred over standard-size chocolate chips. They're delicate, like sprinkles.

## MAKES ABOUT 20–25 TRUFFLES

4 soft Medjool dates, pitted

1 cup (185 g) cooked quinoa, room temperature or cold*

½ cup (129 g) natural peanut butter

¼ cup (85 g) honey

2 cups (160 g) mini chocolate chip morsels

*Approximately ¼ cup (40 g) dry quinoa yields 1 cup (185 g) cooked. For more information on cooking quinoa, see page 149.*

TIP: As an alternative to peanut butter, substitute with almond butter or cashew butter instead. Save leftover pitted dates for smoothies blended with frozen banana, your choice of milk (regular or nut milk) and a dash of cinnamon.

Check your fridge to see if there's space for a small tray or plate; the truffles will need room to chill. Line the tray or plate with parchment paper to prevent sticking.

If your dates are dry and crackly, soak in warm water until soft and pliable. Remove the pits. Quick Tip: Dates are an important binding agent in this recipe. When dried out, the filling won't come together properly.

To a food processor, add the quinoa, dates, peanut butter and honey. Blend until the mixture becomes creamy and smooth (the quinoa will disappear). Stop the machine and scrape down the sides of the bowl—get every last bit!

Chill the filling (in the food processor bowl) for about 10 minutes. It will be easier to scoop. Pour the mini chocolate chips into a bowl.

Using a mini ice cream scoop, about 1 inch (2.5 cm) in diameter, portion the filling into the chocolate chips. Roll around to coat. Place on your lined tray (or plate). Refrigerate for about 45 minutes to 1 hour to set. The truffles should hold together well, and will remain soft and creamy inside. If you're impatient like me, check back after 30 minutes to sample.

Store your truffles in the fridge, in an airtight container for up to 1 week.

*chapter eight*

# FREEZER MARINADES

To marinate something isn't difficult; it's *remembering* to marinate that's the hard part.

Here's my solution: When meat goes on sale, stock up and assemble several bags of marinades to fill your freezer. Do this right when you come home from the store so you don't forget. The meat will absorb the marinade as it freezes and then again as it defrosts. This is one of my favorite kitchen tricks.

In this section, you'll learn how to prepare two versatile marinades, with delicious recipes on how to use them. Some favorites include my super easy One-Pan Sticky Soy Baked Chicken (page 180) and The New Mediterranean Baked Chicken (page 172). Freezer marinades have become an essential part of my shortcut routine and make life easier when you have absolutely zero plans for dinner—simply defrost, cook and serve. It's a no-brainer.

Just don't forget to take the marinades *out* of the freezer....

# LEMON & HERB MARINADE

GLUTEN-FREE OPTION

Fresh and zesty, this marinade is excellent for chicken, beef and fish. The soy sauce adds wonderful depth of flavor.

## MAKES ABOUT ⅓ CUP (150 ML)

Zest and juice of 2 lemons

2 tbsp (30 ml) soy sauce (or tamari for gluten-free)

¼ cup (60 ml) vegetable oil

2–3 cloves of garlic, smashed

Large handful of fresh rosemary or oregano sprigs*

A few turns of freshly ground black pepper

*Substitute 1 tablespoon (3 g) dried rosemary or oregano, if preferred.*

Place all of the ingredients into a large zip-top bag. Mix well to combine. Add the meat, squeezing out as much air as possible. Label and date accordingly. Place directly into the freezer; the protein will absorb the marinade as it begins to freeze and again, as it defrosts. Store up to 3 months.

When space permits, freeze the marinade bags flat like a book. They will defrost more quickly this way and are easier to stack.

TIPS: Freezer marinades work best with protein only, about 1½–2 pounds (680–907 g). Double or triple for larger quantities.

To avoid unfriendly bacteria, do not freeze previously frozen meat, shrimp or fish.

To quickly defrost meat, submerge into a bowl of cold water or microwave.

# THE NEW MEDITERRANEAN BAKED CHICKEN

## GLUTEN-FREE OPTION

This is the most popular recipe on my blog. It's a one-pan chicken bake packed with juicy tomatoes, fresh mozzarella and plenty of fresh, fragrant herbs. I've updated the original instructions to include my zesty Lemon & Herb Marinade (page 171), cooked-bean shortcut and simplified the cooking steps. That means you can make this delicious Mediterranean meal faster.

### SERVES 4–6

2 lbs (907 g) Lemon & Herb marinated boneless, skinless chicken thighs (page 171), defrosted*

Coarse salt and freshly ground black pepper

1 small red onion, thinly sliced

1 pint (284 g) whole cherry tomatoes

1 (6-oz [170-g]) jar marinated artichoke hearts, drained and cut into quarters

1 tbsp (15 ml) olive oil, plus more for drizzling

¼ cup (45 g) roughly chopped kalamata olives

1 cup (177 g) cooked cannellini beans, rinsed and drained**

1 (8-oz [227-g]) tub marinated mini-mozzarella, drained

¼ cup (15 g) roughly chopped parsley

2 tbsp (8 g) basil leaves, cut into ribbons

*If possible, remove the marinade from the fridge 30 minutes prior to cooking to take the chill off.*

**For more information on cooking dried cannellini beans, see pages 109–111, or substitute with half a 15-ounce (425-g) can of cannellini beans.*

Preheat your oven to 400°F (200°C). Line a rimmed baking sheet with parchment paper for easy cleanup.

Remove the chicken from its marinade and pat with paper towels. Cut the chicken into quarters, about 1½ inches (3.8 cm) thick. Season with salt and pepper and place on the sheet pan.

To a large bowl, add the red onion, cherry tomatoes and artichokes. Add the olive oil and season with salt and pepper. Place onto the sheet pan.

Roast for about 30 minutes or so, or until the chicken is cooked through and the tomatoes begin to burst. Give it a quick stir at the 15-minute mark. It will smell wonderful.

Right before serving, add the olives, beans and mozzarella to the pan. Heat through for only a minute; you don't want the cheese to melt all over the place. Top with parsley, basil leaves and a drizzle of extra olive oil for flavor.

TIP: Add any leftovers to whole-grain pasta for a delicious, round two dinner.

# SHEET PAN HONEY-MUSTARD-GLAZED SALMON WITH GREEN BEANS

GLUTEN-FREE OPTION

Adding a honey mustard glaze will wonderfully diversify your Lemon & Herb Marinade (page 171). It's easy enough to do and, if you like the flavor, experiment with chicken or pork as well. Use country mustard instead of purchasing both whole-grain and Dijon mustard—it's a cool trick. And because this recipe is cooked together on a sheet pan, scatter green beans around the fish for an instant side dish; they're ready at the same time.

Alternatively, or in addition, try this glazed salmon with my Simple Radish & Avocado Salad (page 137) and Weeknight Lemon Brown Rice (page 161).

SERVES 4

**HONEY MUSTARD GLAZE**

4 tbsp (62 g) country mustard

2 tbsp (42 g) honey

1½ lbs (680 g) Lemon & Herb marinated salmon fillets (page 171), cut into 4 pieces, defrosted*

Coarse salt and freshly ground black pepper

1 lb (454 g) green beans, ends trimmed

Zest of 1 lemon

1 tbsp (15 ml) olive oil

*If possible, remove the marinade from the fridge about 30 minutes prior to cooking to take the chill off.*

Preheat your oven to 425°F (220°C). Line a rimmed baking sheet with parchment paper for easy cleanup.

In a small bowl, whisk the glaze ingredients together until thoroughly combined.

Remove the salmon from its marinade and pat dry with a paper towel to remove any excess liquid. Place on your baking sheet and season with salt and pepper. Spoon some of the glaze over the top.

In a bowl, toss the green beans with lemon zest and olive oil to coat. Season with salt and pepper. Scatter the green beans all around the tray. Cut the lemon you zested earlier into slices and place on top of the fish.

Bake for about 10 to 12 minutes or until the salmon is fully cooked. The fish should be firm but easily flake apart when poked with a fork. The green beans will be perfectly roasted. Quick Tip: If you like your salmon medium, or medium rare, shorten the cooking time to about 7–10 minutes.

Serve directly on the sheet pan for a casual, rustic-style dinner.

TIP: It's best to use regular green beans instead of skinny haricots verts; they will overcook at the 10–12-minute mark. Or if you prefer, throw them in 5–6 minutes before the fish is done.

# SWEET & SAVORY SOY MARINADE

## GLUTEN-FREE OPTION

As the name suggests, this marinade is the perfect blend of salty and sweet. The red wine vinegar adds acidity for balance. Try with chicken, beef and pork.

## MAKES ABOUT 1 CUP (237 ML)

¼ cup (60 ml) soy sauce (or tamari for gluten-free)

¼ cup (60 ml) ketchup

¼ cup (60 ml) vegetable oil

¼ cup (55 g) brown sugar

2 tbsp (30 ml) red wine vinegar

2–3 cloves of garlic, smashed

Place all of the ingredients into a large zip-top bag. Mix well to combine. Add the meat, squeezing out as much air as possible. Label and date accordingly. Place directly into the freezer; the protein will absorb the marinade as it begins to freeze and again, as it defrosts. Store up to 3 months.

When space permits, freeze the marinade bags flat like a book. They will defrost more quickly this way and are easier to stack.

TIPS: Freezer marinades work best with protein only, about 1½–2 pounds (680–907 g). Double or triple for larger quantities.

To avoid unfriendly bacteria, do not freeze previously frozen meat, shrimp or fish.

To quickly defrost meat, submerge into a bowl of cold water or microwave.

# SWEET & SAVORY SOY GRILLED FLANK STEAK & ZUCCHINI

## GLUTEN-FREE OPTION

Flank steak begs to be marinated. This particular cut can be tough on its own, but when bathed in flavorful honey and soy it willingly transforms into succulent steak. To make the most of your time, throw thin planks of zucchini on the grill for a quick side dish. It's an excellent match.

## SERVES 4–6, DEPENDING ON HOW RAVENOUS YOU ARE

4 medium zucchini

2 tbsp (30 ml) vegetable oil

Coarse salt and freshly ground black pepper

1½ lbs (680 g) Sweet & Savory Soy marinated flank steak (page 176), defrosted*

*If possible, remove the marinade from the fridge 30 minutes prior to cooking to take the chill off.

Preheat your grill to medium-high heat.

Cut the zucchini lengthwise into 1-inch (2.5-cm) planks. Coat with vegetable oil and season with salt and pepper.

Remove the flank steak from its marinade and place on the grill. Cook for about 5 to 6 minutes per side for medium rare, 7 to 10 minutes for medium to medium well. Flank steak is best when cooked medium rare, but a little longer won't turn it into shoe leather. Transfer the steak to a cutting board to rest while you grill the zucchini.

Grill the zucchini for about 4 to 5 minutes per side depending on thickness. The planks should be tender but still hold their shape when ready. The zucchini will continue to cook once removed from the heat.

To serve, thinly slice the meat against the grain. Arrange on a nice platter or serving board with your grilled zucchini on the side.

TIP: For an alternate cooking method, try broiling your flank steak. Position your oven rack to fit the top third and line a rimmed baking sheet with foil. Broil the steak for about 6–8 minutes for medium rare. Rest 5 minutes before slicing.

# ONE-PAN STICKY SOY BAKED CHICKEN

GLUTEN-FREE OPTION

I used to work as a private chef and babysitter for a family in NYC. They had three adorable kids. Feeding them was always a challenge, as little kids can be quite honest with their criticism—they let me have it! Luckily, their pint-size palettes approved of this dish. It's so easy to prepare—place both the chicken and marinade in a dish and bake for about 35–40 minutes. That's it. The marinade doubles as a sweet and sticky sauce.

SERVES 4

4½ lbs (1.9 kg) Sweet & Savory Soy marinated whole chicken (page 176), cut into 8 pieces, defrosted* (see tips)

1 tbsp (4 g) roughly chopped parsley

*If possible, remove the marinade from the fridge 30 minutes prior to cooking to take the chill off.*

Position your oven racks to fit the top third portion. Preheat your oven to 425°F (220°C). Grab a 9 x 13-inch (23 x 33-cm) or 13.5 x 11-inch (34 x 28-cm) baking dish.

Add the chicken and marinade to the baking dish. Make sure to arrange the chicken in one single layer, skin side up.

Bake in the oven, top rack for about 35 to 40 minutes, or until the chicken is cooked through. To crisp the skin, broil for 1 to 2 minutes watching it closely (you don't want it to burn).

Before serving, transfer the chicken to a cutting board. Carefully pour the pan sauce into a Pyrex measuring jug or gravy separator and wait for the residual fat to rise to the surface. Spoon it off and discard. Quick Tip: This step is optional if using skinless chicken.

Add the chicken back to the pan and pour the sweet and sticky sauce on top. Sprinkle with choppped parsley, to serve.

TIPS: You will have to double the marinade recipe to accommodate 1 whole chicken.

If you're good at quartering a chicken, now is the time to show off your skills. If not, purchase a whole chicken cut into 8 pieces.

# 7-6-5 PORK TENDERLOIN WITH GRILLED ONION SALAD

GLUTEN-FREE OPTION

Ever wonder how to grill pork tenderloin properly? This method is fool-proof. It's brought to you by FineCookingMagazine.com and I've been using it for years. The numbers 7-6-5 signify the amount of cooking time for the pork, yielding reliable results every time. It's brilliant.

Pork tenderloin is naturally juicy, and my Sweet & Savory Soy Marinade (page 176) makes it even more flavorful. Grill sweet onions alongside the pork and toss with greens for a quick and healthy salad.

## SERVES 4

1½ lbs (680 g) Sweet & Savory Soy marinated pork tenderloin (page 176), defrosted*

1 large onion, such as Vidalia or red onion

2 tsp (10 ml) vegetable oil

Coarse salt and freshly ground black pepper

### BALSAMIC-DIJON JAM JAR DRESSING

1 tsp Dijon mustard

1 tbsp (15 ml) balsamic vinegar

¼ cup (60 ml) red wine vinegar

½ cup (118 ml) olive oil

Coarse salt and freshly ground black pepper

4 large handfuls of baby greens

1 cup (150 g) cherry tomatoes, halved

*If possible, remove the marinade from the fridge 30 minutes prior to cooking to take the chill off.*

Preheat your outdoor grill to high heat.

Remove the pork tenderloin from its marinade and place onto a cutting board.

Cut the onion into thick slices, keeping the rings intact. Lightly coat with vegetable oil. Season with salt and pepper.

Place the pork on the grill. Close the lid and cook for about 7 minutes. After 7 minutes, flip over the pork. Close the lid again and cook for an additional 6 minutes. Turn the burners off. Keep the lid closed and let the pork rest on the grill for 5 minutes. Transfer to a cutting board.

While the pork is resting, use that time to grill the onions. Adjust the heat to medium and grill the onions about 4 to 5 minutes per side, or until soft. Transfer to a cutting board and give them a rough chop.

For the dressing, combine the first four ingredients in an empty jam jar. Season with salt and pepper. Screw the lid on tight and shake well to blend.

Add the baby greens, cherry tomatoes and onions to a large bowl. Toss lightly with the dressing.

To serve, slice the pork into rounds and place on a large serving platter. Arrange your beautiful grilled onion salad on the side.

*chapter nine*

# INSTEAD OF WHITE WINE

I never thought I'd run into this problem, really.

There's always something of interest to drink in our house. But what happens when you're out of white wine and there's Quick Shrimp Scampi (page 188) to be made? Some say to leave it out altogether, which of course you can do in the recipes to follow. But I'm going to let you in on a little secret: *dry white vermouth*. It's not just for cocktails, it's a brilliant shortcut.

White vermouth is a fortified wine, infused with a botanical blend of herbs, flowers and other aromatics. Because it lasts up to two months in the fridge, there's no need to run out to the store for a bottle of white wine, which comparatively speaking, only lasts about three days when opened. Save yourself the trip!

Not only that, you'll waste less. How many times have you opened a bottle of white wine only to use half a cup (118 ml)? What happens to the rest of the bottle if you don't drink it? Adopting white vermouth as a time-saving shortcut will allow you to use only what you need, when you need it.

When choosing white vermouth look for something inexpensive yet good enough to drink (just ask if you're unsure). A small bottle will cost about $5. It has a stronger alcohol content than white wine, so you'll inevitably use less.

# 30-MINUTE CHICKEN PICCATA

Watching my mom make this dish over the years, I've learned that chicken piccata is all about organization. While the chicken browns, use that time to prep the rest of your ingredients: Dice the shallots, open the vermouth (have a sip, obviously) and slice your lemons to serve. This way, you will be one step ahead of the game, with less stress.

## SERVES 4

½ cup (63 g) + 1 tsp flour, divided

1½ lbs (680 g) thin sliced chicken cutlets

Coarse salt and freshly ground black pepper

2 tbsp (30 ml) olive oil

¼ cup (40 g) shallots, diced

2 tbsp (17 g) brined capers, rinsed

2 tbsp (8 g) roughly chopped parsley

½ lemon, sliced, for garnish

2 tbsp (30 g) Garlic Butter (page 63), or 2 tbsp (30 g) unsalted butter + 1 clove of garlic, grated

¼ cup (60 ml) dry white vermouth

1½ cups (355 ml) Triple-Duty Chicken Stock (page 27)

Juice of ½ lemon

Lemon slices, for serving

Add ½ cup (63 g) of flour to a shallow bowl. Reserve the remaining 1 teaspoon for the sauce. Season the chicken on both sides with salt and pepper. Dredge in flour, shaking off any excess as you go.

In a large, 12-inch (30-cm) skillet, warm the olive oil over medium-low heat. Working in batches, brown the chicken, about 3 minutes per side. Transfer to a plate.

Meanwhile, prep the rest of your ingredients: Dice the shallots, rinse your capers, chop the parsley and cut the lemon into slices.

Add the garlic butter to the pan. Sauté the shallots over low heat, about 30 seconds.

In a mixing bowl, add the reserved 1 teaspoon of flour, vermouth and chicken stock. Whisk well to dissolve the flour. Pour the liquid into the pan, scraping up any brown bits stuck to the bottom. Bring the sauce to a boil, and simmer until reduced by half. The sauce should look slightly thickened.

Add the capers, lemon juice and parsley to the pan. Add back the chicken and any accumulated juices. Taste, and season with extra lemon juice, salt and pepper.

To serve, transfer the chicken to a large serving platter and spoon the delicious sauce over the top. Garnish with lemon slices.

# QUICK SHRIMP SCAMPI WITH WHOLE-GRAIN COUSCOUS

Traditionally, white wine is used for shrimp scampi to deglaze the pan and to add flavor to the sauce. But here, I use dry white vermouth instead; it pairs beautifully with seafood as does rich garlic butter and citrusy lemon. I even add a splash of stock to stretch out the sauce because really, that's what it's all about!

PS: Using Garlic Butter (page 63) will make this dish come together even faster, but if you don't have any, I've included the proportions below.

SERVES 4

1 cup (173 g) whole-grain couscous, dry

2 tbsp (30 ml) olive oil

4 tbsp (60 g) Garlic Butter (page 63), or 4 tbsp (60 g) of unsalted butter + 2 cloves of garlic, grated

1½ (680 g) pounds peeled and deveined shrimp, tail on

Coarse salt and freshly ground black pepper

¼ cup (60 ml) dry white vermouth

½ cup (118 ml) Triple-Duty Chicken Stock (page 27)

2 tbsp (8 g) finely chopped parsley

1 lemon, cut into wedges

Bring a medium-size pot of water to a boil. Cook the couscous according to the package instructions. When finished, add the olive oil and fluff with a fork to separate the grains. Keep warm.

In a large, 12-inch (30-cm) skillet, warm the garlic butter over low heat. Be careful not to burn the garlic; the sauce will taste bitter.

Add the shrimp to the pan. Season lightly with salt and pepper. Increase the heat to medium and sauté, stirring occasionally, until the shrimp are bright pink, about 2–4 minutes.

To deglaze, remove the pan from the heat to avoid flare up. Reduce the heat to low. Pour in the white vermouth and chicken stock. Place the pan back on the stove, increase the heat and continue to cook until the sauce is slightly reduced, about 1 minute. Sprinkle with parsley.

To serve, place the couscous onto a serving platter. Add the shrimp, spooning some of the delicious buttery sauce over the top. Tuck in some lemon wedges on the side and enjoy.

# RAINBOW BRAISED CARROTS

GLUTEN-FREE

My go-to preparation for carrots is usually roasted or eaten raw, but they're sweet and tender when braised. Combined with white vermouth and thyme, this is an easy side dish to accompany any meal. I used a mix of purple, yellow and orange carrots, but a regular bunch of orange carrots will work too. This would be lovely with parsnips and other root vegetables for variety.

## SERVES 4, AS A SIDE DISH

1 lb (454 g) carrots, assorted colors

2 tbsp (30 ml) dry white vermouth

¼ cup (60 ml) Triple-Duty Chicken Stock (page 27)

2 small sprigs of thyme

Coarse salt and freshly ground black pepper

1 tbsp (21 g) honey

2 tbsp (30 g) unsalted butter

¼ cup (15 g) roughly chopped parsley

Juice of ½ lemon

To begin, trim and peel your carrots. Cut them into quarters. If you find that your carrots are very tapered, simply quarter the top half and then leave the bottom portion whole. This way, they will cook evenly.

In a large, 12-inch (30-cm) skillet, add the carrots, vermouth, chicken stock and thyme sprigs over low heat. Season with salt and pepper.

Place the lid on top and simmer for about 20–25 minutes or until the carrots are tender. To check for doneness, insert a small paring knife into one of the carrots; if it slides out easily, they're ready. If there's resistance, cook for additional time.

Drizzle the honey over the carrots. Add the butter. Crank up the heat to medium, and reduce the sauce to a glaze, about 1 minute. The carrots should look nice and shiny.

Right before serving, stir in your chopped parsley and squeeze some lemon over the top to brighten the flavor.

TIP: Peeling carrots is a messy job. Instead of working over a bowl or directly on your countertop, peel the carrots over a sheet of parchment paper. When you're done, just pick up the whole thing and throw it out (or reuse for something else). Works great with potato peels too.

# 7-MINUTE MUSSELS

Mussels are a home cook's best-kept secret! They are incredibly easy to prepare—just throw them in a pot and steam. It only takes about five to seven minutes, and they're inexpensive too. Here, the mussels bathe in a fragrant combination of white vermouth and shallots, which begs to be mopped up with good, crusty bread. This rivals any restaurant dish, if you ask me.

## SERVES 4, GENEROUSLY

4 lbs (1.8 kg) cultivated mussels

2 shallots, thinly sliced

1 cup (237 ml) dry white vermouth

2 tbsp (30 g) unsalted butter

Good crusty bread, for dunking

To begin, have a look at your mussels. If there are broken pieces or shells that won't close when tapped, immediately discard. Rinse under cold water and scrub as needed.

Tip the mussels into a large pot. Add the shallots, vermouth and butter.

Place the lid on top and set the heat to high. Steam the mussels until their shells open, about 5 to 7 minutes. Discard any mussel shells that do not open.

Gather everyone around the table, and serve the mussels directly in the pot. Enjoy with thick slices of crusty country bread to mop up the delicious broth.

TIP: Fish markets and grocery stores carry cultivated or farmed mussels, which have minimal sand and grit compared with wild. Although these mussels are considerably cleaner, they still need to be rinsed and scrubbed. Store mussels over a bowl of ice (uncovered) and refrigerate until ready to use.

# SIMPLE BAKED FISH WITH LEMON & OLIVES

Oh yes, this is good. Choose any firm fish that you'd like, such as cod or halibut (salmon would work too) and bake in the oven with white vermouth, citrusy lemon and briny olives. This easy and delicious dinner only takes about 30 minutes. Top with seasoned breadcrumbs for the perfect crunchy crust.

### SERVES 4

2 tbsp (30 g) unsalted butter, plus more for coating

1½ lbs (680 g) center-cut white fish, such as cod or halibut

2 tbsp (30 ml) olive oil

Zest of 1 lemon, juice reserved

1 clove of garlic, grated

1 tbsp (2 g) chopped fresh rosemary or oregano leaves

Coarse salt and freshly ground black pepper

⅓ cup (78 ml) dry white vermouth

1 cup (150 g) assorted black and green olives, pitted

#### BREADCRUMB CRUST
¼ cup (30 g) Italian seasoned breadcrumbs

1 tsp olive oil

Lemon wedges, to serve

Chive flowers (optional)

Position the racks to fit the top-third portion of the oven. Preheat to 425°F (220°C). Lightly coat a 9 x 13-inch (23 x 33-cm) baking dish with butter.

Remove the fish from its packaging and pat with paper towels to remove any excess moisture. This will allow the olive oil and herbs to stick to the fish. Into a large bowl, add the olive oil, lemon zest, garlic and rosemary (or oregano) leaves. Roll the fish around in the mixture to coat.

Place the fish in your baking dish, scraping the herb mixture from the bowl into the dish as well. Season with salt and pepper. Add the vermouth and lemon juice from the lemon you zested earlier. Break up the 2 tablespoons (30 g) of butter into pieces and scatter it around the dish. Add the olives.

For the crumb crust, mix the breadcrumbs with olive oil in a small bowl; the crust will brown more evenly this way. Top each fish with the breadcrumbs, patting down gently as you go.

Bake for about 15 to 20 minutes. The fish should be firm, yet slightly flaky when probed with a fork.

Remove from the oven and serve with lemon wedges. Sprinkle with chive flowers, if using.

# HONEY ROASTED WHITE PEACHES

GLUTEN-FREE — VEGETARIAN

Even in July, when it's 100°F (38°C) outside, I will happily turn the oven on to make these roasted peaches. The sweetness of white peaches complements the floral notes of vermouth and honey (I sound like a sommelier, no?). Yellow peaches or a combo of both will work too.

For best results, make sure that your peaches are ripe but still firm. This way the fruit won't disintegrate when baked. Spoon the warm honeyed syrup over the peaches, and top with crème fraîche or vanilla ice cream.

SERVES 4–6

4 white or yellow peaches

¼ cup (60 ml) white vermouth

¼ cup (85 g) honey

1 vanilla bean or ½ tsp vanilla extract

2 tbsp (30 g) unsalted butter

Thick dollops of crème fraîche or vanilla ice cream (optional)

Preheat your oven to 400°F (200°C). Select a baking dish large enough to fit the peaches.

Add the vermouth and honey to the baking dish. If using a vanilla bean, slice it in half lengthwise and scrape out the seeds with the tip of a spoon. Add to the dish and whisk well to combine. You will have the beginnings of a lovely, fragrant sauce.

Slice the peaches in half and remove the stone. Place into your baking dish, cut side up. Break the butter into pieces and top each peach half.

Bake for about 20 minutes. The peaches should be soft, but still hold their shape when ready.

Serve warm, with extra sauce over the top and dollops of crème fraîche or ice cream, if desired.

TIP: Save leftover vanilla pods to make homemade vanilla sugar. Submerge in 1 cup (200 g) of sugar and store in an airtight container up to 1 year.

# THANK YOU

Writing a cookbook takes a team of extraordinary people. I am forever grateful to those who helped make my ultimate dream possible.

To my readers, seen and unseen: You are the inspiration and motivation to continue on this journey. I read every single one of your comments and emails. *You* are what drives me to create.

My boys, Dillon and Jake: I love you so much my heart could burst! Thank you for not burning the house down while Mommy spent countless hours photographing everything in sight. Everything I do is for you.

To my husband, Johan: You made it all possible. From my first camera to supplying me with chocolate-covered espresso beans to wrangling our little boys, the sweetness of your love and support sings in my heart. Always.

To my parents: Mom, thank you for dedicating your Saturdays and being my all-around assistant (wait, you don't like mopping floors?). You are my biggest cheerleader! Dad, thank you for being wonderfully supportive, playing with the kids and always having a pot of coffee ready to go. The herbs that you grew for this book are beautiful.

My wonderful family and friends: Thank you for letting me raid your cabinets for interesting plates and spoons; thank you for completing strange and unusual tasks like cooking sweet potatoes or slow-cooking a pot of beans as per my request; and most of all thank you for enticing me with wine at the finish line.

To Mimi, Grandpa and Grandma: Your recipes are kept in a beautiful wooden box on my desk. They sat there the entire time I worked on this project. Although you will never hold this book in your hands, your inspiration comes through my words and photos. I know you know.

To Auntie Connie: You are my legal rock and an incredible aunt! Thank you for everything that you do.

To Laura: Who would've thought a casual conversation at the kitchen table would turn into a blog? Thank you for your encouragement and most of all, for proofreading my blog posts. You are the best.

To my brilliant recipe testers: I can't thank you enough for heeding my call to action! Your time, enthusiasm and support is overwhelmingly heartwarming. Huge hugs to every single one of you (in random order) Justine Barnabo, Claire Beach, Elise Ingenito, Laura McGorty, Donika Oran, Lynette Moore, Beverley Hart Press, Diane Baker, Ann McMurtrie Fulton, Justine Fontinell, Danielle Dorward, Ann Krause, Laney Sachs, Traci York, Ally Phillips, Patti Veneziano and family, and Celia Callow (with Priscilla, the sourdough starter).

To my local suppliers: Golden Earthworm Organic Farm (www.goldenearthworm.com) and Good Water Farms (www.goodwaterfarms.com). Keep sprinkling your magic onto the Earth. Your produce is vibrant, full of energy and an absolute dream to work with.

To the wonderful team at Page Street Publishing: Will and Sarah, thank you for believing in me and bringing my story to life. This has been such a fun and exciting project. Meg, thank you for your beautiful book design.

# ABOUT THE AUTHOR

EMILIE RAFFA is a food writer, self-taught photographer and a cook who was classically trained at the International Culinary Center. Her blog, The Clever Carrot, focuses on healthy comfort food. As a busy mom, Emilie's humor and down-to-earth style takes us on a visual journey tantalizing our senses and inspiring the art of homemade cooking.

Emilie's work has been featured online on The Huffington Post, Food 52, Saveur, Food & Wine, TODAY Food and in the pages of *Artful Blogging* magazine. She was a finalist for "best food photography" in the annual Saveur Blog Awards and is an editor for the digital cooking publication, feedfeed. Emilie lives on Long Island with her husband and two little boys. Oftentimes, she can be found folding laundry and dreaming about her next meal....

www.theclevercarrot.com

# CATEGORY INDEX

GF = GLUTEN FREE OR GLUTEN FREE OPTION  ·  VG = VEGETARIAN  ·  V = VEGAN

# INDEX

GF = GLUTEN FREE OR GLUTEN FREE OPTION · VG = VEGETARIAN · V = VEGAN